Jay and Jeannie Levinson's

Startup
Guide
to
GUERRILLA
MARKETING

A Simple
Battle Plan
for First-Time
Marketers

WITHDRAWN

EP
Entrepreneur.
Press

Publisher: Jere L. Calmes
Cover Design: Beth Hansen-Winter
Production and Composition: Eliot House Productions

Library of Congress Cataloging-in-Publication Data
  Levinson, Jay Conrad.
    Startup guide to guerrilla marketing: a simple battle plan for first-time marketers/by Jay Conrad Levinson and Jeannie Levinson.
      p.   cm.
    A prequel to their best-selling Guerrilla marketing.
    ISBN 1-59918-153-3 (alk. paper)
    ISBN 13: 9781599181530
    1. Marketing. 2. Entrepreneurship--Psychological aspects. 3. Marketing—Management. 4. Small business—Management. I. Levinson, Jeannie. II. Levinson, Jay Conrad. Guerilla marketing. III. Title.
  HF5415.L47965 2007
  658.8—dc22   2007035739

Printed in Canada
12 11 10 09 08   10 9 8 7 6 5 4 3 2

CONTENTS

ACKNOWLEDGMENTS

Our primary and sole acknowledgement goes to Mark Langley, the solid gold guerrilla marketer who helped us buy the house we now own. He demonstrated all the attitudes and attributes we would pray to find in a real estate expert, and took two years to find exactly what these guerrillas ordered and get a healthy start-up in a new home in a brand new town

Our book owes a ton of gratitude to Mark.

—Jay and Jeannie Levinson

People Are Saying

"Forget the retired business executives with the firm handshakes and the sincere eye contact. Forget the SBA. Forget the seminar speakers with the expensive haircuts and the million-dollar smiles. If you want the best, most proven, most widely used and easiest-to-implement advice in the world on how to market a start-up business, go no further than Jay and Jeannie Levinson's new book. They know what really works, and you need to know what they are so generously willing to share with you."

—DAVID GARFINKEL, AUTHOR OF *ADVERTISING HEADLINES THAT MAKE YOU RICH*

"If you are starting a business on a tight budget, this book is for you! The Father of Guerrilla Marketing reveals dozens of high impact, low-cost strategies for getting new customers using time, energy, and imagination. If you want to start making money from your new business, get this book!"

—MITCH MEYERSON, FOUNDER OF GUERRILLA MARKETING COACHING

"Guidance for new marketers, reminders for experienced ones, and useful tips for everyone. I educate individuals on how to build businesses that will succeed and last, I know first-hand that marketing is key for any entrepreneur. I am so thrilled that Jay and Jeannie have written this fabulous book sharing their expert knowledge. I have seen personally, their incredible results, they have proven to be the best of the best in guerilla marketing. You need to read this book today; adopting this mindset, it will be difficult for you to not be successful. They are the BEST at the game!"

—LORAL LANGEMEIER, *THE MILLIONAIRE MAKER*, CEO AND FOUNDER OF LIVE OUT LOUD, INC.

PREFACE

Running your own business is an armload of responsibilities. Marketing your company is still another Everest-sized bump in the road you must surmount. If you market with less than the skill of a guerrilla, you poison your business and your future. If you know what the guerrilla knows, marketing gives your business vigor and immortality,

Although precious few know this, there actually is a way to assure that you'll market the right way and attain the profits that are the fruits of guerrilla marketing.

That way is to start in the right place. Many business owners start out in the wrong direction, doomed to become a depressing statistic in reports of the 50 percent of small businesses that fail the first year and the 95 percent that fail within the first five years. Many of these now forgotten companies had the goods to carry them to greatness. But they didn't have the marketing savvy.

There are so many businesses just like those that are now sad memories that we wrote this book to set those ventures on the right course before it's too late. In these pages, we stand behind them, take them by the shoulders, gently cradle their heads, aim them in the right direction, then give them a nudge and watch entrepreneurial gravity go to work.

Some of these companies are at the starting line or nearing it. Other companies are already in the race, giving it their all. All these companies can benefit bigtime from the guidance offered in this book.

Are successful guerrilla entrepreneurs born or made? Both is the right answer. You'll learn the answer about yourself in a few pages and you'll discover a few minor changes you can make to bring about major results. By results, we refer to an increase in your profits and your free time. That's our goal with this book. If it's yours, too, you've hitched to the right star.

As you go deeper into the exhilarating options for marketing your business in true guerrilla fashion, you'll walk the walk as we talk the talk. You'll learn about a guerrilla marketing strategy, plan one, then create one that you'll be able to use for the next one to ten years.

The ease and the wisdom that went into that strategy will easily translate into the guerrilla marketing calendar you create to guide you through the up and down days of a high-energy economy and put you in control—a rare experience for many business owners.

You'll see just how you must proceed to get the most from the internet—a giant until you realize that it's a pussycat in disguise. We'll help you get cozy with the internet because it now ranks up there with oxygen, water, and sunlight.

We figure that our Guerrilla Marketing books will be a whole lot more valuable to readers now that they can start at the start as you're about to do.

1

WHERE
TO START

We have good news and better news about guerrilla marketing. The good news is that you're already at the starting point with this page of this book. The better news is that it gets easier and more fun as you continue on through the remaining pages.

A solid and successful guerrilla marketing attack has a beginning and a middle, but if you're doing it right, it has no ending. The beginning is right here and right now, when you develop the mindset of a guerrilla. The middle is when you breathe life into all the tactics of a profitable campaign. The ending never happens, unless you decide to sell your business or tire of endless profits.

Because we want you to partake of those endless profits, we want you to get off to a running start. The way to do that is to have the personality of a successful guerrilla marketer. If you don't have that personality yet,

> A solid and successful guerrilla marketing attack has a beginning and a middle, but if you're doing it right, it has no ending.

we'll show you just how to develop it. You also need to have special attributes—the kind possessed by guerrilla marketers basking in success. The way to get those attributes is to be born with them or to generate them yourself—something we'll teach you to do in the upcoming pages.

You also need the right attitudes. Without them, you're sunk before you begin. With them, you're already poised for victory and destined for success. How do you get those winning attitudes? You're doing it already by reading the words on these pages, then acting on the information we'll be giving to you.

We don't want you to think that guerrilla marketing is easy, because it isn't easy. But we do want you to know that once you have the personality, the attributes, and the attitudes of a guerrilla, it's hard to fail. It's tough to be anything but successful with the mindset of a guerrilla. And it's kind of amazing that you can get that mindset simply by reading about it in a book. Yet, that's precisely why we've written this book—to give you that mindset, then set you on your way.

To do that, you've got to know what marketing really is—because it's certainly not what most people think it is. You also must know exactly what guerrilla marketing is. And since we're devoted to making you a master of guerrilla marketing, we'll make sure that you know just what you're mastering. If you have any questions, you won't have once you've completed this book. Trust us on that one.

> Once you have the personality, the attributes, and the attitudes of a guerrilla, it's hard to fail.

You're about to launch and succeed with a guerrilla marketing attack. It's a ten-step process, and we'll guide you through it every step of the way. We'll tell you the research you must do. That part is crucial, easy, and actually enjoyable. We'll show you how to create a benefits list so that you know clearly what makes you so good and can communicate that goodness to your target audience.

Do you know what a meme is? It's an extremely simple way to communicate an entire idea instantly. Picture a hitchhiker standing there with his thumb out. You don't need an instruction manual to show you what he wants you to do. What he's doing is using a meme to get you to take a specific action. We'll get into the nitty and the gritty of how you can create a meme to get people to see things your way.

There are 200 marketing weapons that you can use to earn the profits you dream about. The majority of those weapons don't cost a cent. Yet they're all true weapons of mass profitability. What are the weapons? Which are best for you? Now that we've asked those questions, you can count on us answering them for you.

Of course, to breathe life into our own dreams for you, you're going to have to operate with a plan. We'll take you by the hand, and show you how to create a plan that will work for you. It'll be only seven sentences long, but don't let its brevity mislead you about its power and potency.

To achieve all the financial greatness that we have in store for you, the timing has got to be perfect. How can you make that happen? With a guerrilla marketing calendar—just like the one we'll show you how to create for yourself.

Take comfort in the knowledge that you won't be fighting the guerrilla marketing battles by yourself. Far from it. Naturally, you've got us as your partners. But we'll also show you how to get a lot more allies through what we call your fusion marketing partners. There are more of them out there than you think. How to enlist them in your guerrilla army is paramount to your success. That's why we'll show you exactly how.

Once you're armed with all those guerrilla marketing necessities, it's time to launch your guerrilla marketing attack. Doing that will be one of the most rewarding parts of your life in business. We'll show you how to make it extra rewarding. The hard stuff comes next. It's maintaining your attack. But that won't be very difficult for you because you'll know exactly what to expect and how to sidestep the tough parts.

Keeping track of all your efforts is very important to us and even more important to you. How to do it? The upcoming pages reveal the

> A meme is an extremely simple way to communicate an entire idea instantly.

12 DIFFERENCES BETWEEN GUERRILLA WANNA-BE'S AND TRUE GUERRILLA ENTREPRENEURS

1. Wanna-be's obsess about ideas.

   Guerrilla Entrepreneurs obsess about implementation.

2. Wanna-be's want more web traffic.

   Guerrilla Enrepreneurs focus on sales conversion.

3. Wanna-be's focus on positive thinking.

   Guerrilla Entrepreneurs plan for multiple contingencies.

4. Wanna-be's want to get on TV and get "famous."

   Guerrilla Entrepreneurs build their list.

5. Wanna-be's seek a perfect plan.

   Guerrilla Entrepreneurs execute—and adjust the plan later.

6. Wanna-be's wait for their lucky break.

   Guerrilla Entrepreneurs engineer four, five, six plans and execute them in tandem, wagering that at least one plan will get traction.

7. Wanna-be's fear looking stupid in front of their friends.

   Guerrilla Entrepreneurs willingly risk making fools of themselves, knowing that long-term success is a good trade for short-term loss of dignity.

8. Wanna-be's shield their precious ideas from harsh reality, postponing the verdict of success or failure until "someday."

   Guerrilla Entrepreneurs expose their ideas to cold reality as soon as reasonably possible.

9. Wanna-be's put off practicing basketball until they've got Air Jordans.

   Guerrilla Entrepreneurs practice barefoot behind the garage.

10. Wanna-be's believe what they're told and believe their own assumptions.

    Guerrilla Entrepreneurs do original research and determine what paths have been already trod.

12 DIFFERENCES BETWEEN GUERRILLA WANNA-BE'S AND TRUE GUERRILLA ENTREPRENEURS, continued

11. Wanna-be's believe they can do anything.
    Guerrilla Entrepreneurs do what they're gifted for and delegate the rest.

12. Wanna-be's think about the world in terms of COULD and SHOULD.
    Guerrilla Entrepreneurs think in terms of IS and CAN BE.

answer. There will then come a time when everything is falling into place for you and you're making larger bank deposits than you expected. That's not the time for you to kick back and give yourself a high five. Instead, that's your cue to ramp up all your actions and to improve every single aspect of your marketing. Take heart in the notion that we're here at your side to help you do that. It will be our pleasure.

Now you're ready to enjoy the fruits of your labor and to combine all your newly gained wisdom into an unstoppable profit-earning machine. That will happen when you put all that wisdom together and become a guerrilla who inspires shock and awe.

When that does happen, as it surely will, your guerrilla marketing will be in high gear, your profits will be held in high regard, and you'll be in high spirits. That's because you got off to a great start. Our reward will come in the knowledge that we were there the entire time. And we knew it would happen.

It's going to be better than you think, so let's get going!

THE PERSONALITY OF A GUERRILLA MARKETER

It's going to be an uphill battle leading a guerrilla marketing attack unless you've got certain personality traits. We're sure that you've already got some, if not most, of these traits already. But you need all of them.

While creating marketing programs for many of the largest, wealthiest, and most successful companies on earth, as well as some of the smallest, newest, and most poorly funded, we've studied the leaders of those bound for success—in the quest for personality characteristics that they have in common. We've found an even dozen. Those companies on the *Fortune* 500 and headed for the *Fortune* 500 have had marketing campaigns masterminded by honchos with these twelve traits.

We've looked for exceptions, but have found none. Does that mean that if you have these traits, you'll succeed? It does not. But it does mean that unless you have them, the odds are seriously against you. And that's

Consciously try to develop the personality characteristics that you don't have now.

no way to start any guerrilla marketing venture. By consciously trying to develop the personality characteristics that you don't have now, you'll be putting the odds in your favor, a highly desirable state for any self-respecting guerrilla marketer.

Your goal: to possess all 12 traits. Our goal: to show you how to do that. You probably won't need a personality transplant, but you may need to sharpen some of the rough edges lest they trip you up.

Trait 1: Patience

The identification of this trait began with a study in which researchers were asked a very tough question: "How many times must your message penetrate a person's mind in order to transform them from total apathy, meaning, they've never heard of you, to purchase readiness, which means they're dying to buy from you?" Astonishingly, the researchers came up with an answer. It was *nine*. Your message must penetrate people's minds nine times before they're ready to buy from you. That's the good news. The bad news is that for every three times you put out the word and expose them to your message, they're only paying attention one time. After all, they do have more important things to do with their lives than focus on your marketing.

So you put out the word three times and your message penetrates their mind one time. What happens then? Nothing happens. So you put out the word six times and penetrate their minds two times. What happens then? They faintly realize that they've heard your name before. But that's as far as it goes. Now you put out the word nine times, penetrating their minds three times. What happens then? Something does happen: They realize they've seen or heard your marketing before, and they know that unsuccessful companies don't market. The momentum has started, but they're not even close to buying what you're selling.

Sticking with the drill, you put out the word—by radio, television, newspaper ads, print ads, e-mail, signs, banners, whatever—a total of 12 times, penetrating their minds 4 times. What happens then? Not much. They may look around for other signs of your existence, perhaps even ask a friend about you, but they certainly aren't ready to buy from you yet. You put out the word 15 times, penetrating their minds 5 times. What happens then? Something wonderful happens. They read every word of your copy. They pay close attention to your commercial. If you list your web site—and we sure hope that you do—they click over to it and check you out. If you offer a brochure, they request it. The momentum leading to the sales picks up, but notice, they do not buy from you.

At this point, you begin to feel frustrated. After all, you've peppered your market with powerful messages, but they do not beat a path to your door. It does enter their minds to own what you're selling, but they are just plain not ready to buy from you. Not yet. Maybe never. Here's where most business owners abandon their campaigns. They figure they're doing everything wrong and that they need a new message, new media, a revamped web site. The truth is that they're doing everything right. But marketing just doesn't do what they expected it to do. They expected it to work in a hurry.

Listen up. Marketing does a lot of good things, wonderful things. But one thing it rarely does is work in a hurry. Get serious. Don't be like those companies that decide to forsake their marketing investments and start all over again at square one. We wince at the thought. Doing that is called "sellus interruptus." The sale is never consummated. Here's where you've got to hang in there and continue to put out the word. You put it out there 18 times, penetrating the minds of your increasingly interested prospects 6 times. What happens at that point? They begin to think of when they'll make the purchase, where they'll get the money. But they do not buy.

So you put out the word 21 times, penetrating their minds 7 times. This is when they tell others that they're planning to purchase from you. They may even note it in their datebooks or on their Blackberries. Put out the word 24 times and you've penetrated their minds 8

> Your message must penetrate people's minds nine times before they're ready to buy from you.

times. This is when they check with whomever they usually check with before making big ticket purchases. This is when they actually plan the day and the time that they will buy from you. You see nothing to indicate that they're ready to take the plunge onto your customer list. But you continue marketing, putting out the word 27 times. You've penetrated their minds 9 times. *Nine* times. What happens then? They come in and they buy from you. They treat you like an old friend. You don't know them from Adam or Eve, but you have built up a strong sense of familiarity and familiarity is the factor that breeds sales.

How on earth did you bring about this blessed state of affairs? You did it with patience, the personality trait that opened heaven's doors. Without your patience, it just wouldn't have happened. With patience, it almost always happens. If you don't have patience or can't develop patience, we hope you either leave the marketing department or find another line of work. Patience makes it happen. Some people think that marketing is a miracle worker. Not true. It's patience that works the miracles.

Trait 2: Imagination

This trait may not mean what you think it means. It doesn't necessarily mean the creativity to dream up clever headlines, compelling graphics, zippy copy, or memorable slogans. Instead, it refers to how you contend with reality.

Lots of companies come up with jazzy headlines, graphics, copy, or slogans. If you do, too, you're just one in a large crowd. That kind of imagination will not help you stand out in a crowd. What you need is the kind of imagination that helps you stand apart from the crowd. One more clever headline isn't going to do that for you.

In a jam-packed media environment, you need much more than that. You've got to face more than your competition—and we certainly don't want to undermine them because they're getting smarter

THE GUERRILLA MARKETING FLORIST

This is an example of a true guerrilla spirit: a tiny investment, a huge imagination, and a happy pay-off. People will always spend money to solve a problem before spending to improve something that is already OK. A guerrilla marketing florist knows that this is true in every area of life and not just business-to-business marketing.

After all of the social expressions of the year-end holidays, flower sales can drop off until Valentine's Day. One florist's solution is a small road sign that simply asks, "How mad is she?" He never had a busier January thanks to the sign.

every day. The truth is that you've got to face reality head on and you're got to do something to rise above it. You've got to do something your prospects and customers have never seen before so that you can capture and hold their attention better than any competitor anywhere, anytime.

Let's say you're doing a direct mailing. You certainly won't be the first, but you certainly do want to be the best. How do you do that? By printing something unusual on the envelope? Face it, everybody and their cousin does that. There's no guerrilla genius necessary to come up with a set of words or pictures that will beg the recipient to open their envelope. But guerrillas have the imagination to break through that direct mail clutter and get their mailing noticed, their envelope opened, and their message read. They have the imagination to do something their audience has never seen before and that even you have never seen before.

It begins with their willingness to pop for first-class postage. We're not talking about breaking the bank here. We're only referring to you being willing to invest in 41 cents worth of postage, the cost of a first-class stamp. But you don't buy a 41-cent stamp. Anyone can buy that kind of stamp. You certainly do not use a postage metered stamp because that has "boring" stamped all over it.

Do you invest in a beautiful, brand new commemorative stamp? Too easy, and to be honest, too common. Instead, you take your 41 cents worth of postage and you invest in fourteen stamps. You buy two six-cent stamps, five three-cent stamps, and seven two-cent stamps. That's 14 stamps totaling 41 cents, the same as a regular 41-cent stamp.

You put those 14 stamps on the envelopes, do your mailing, and realize that when the recipients receive their envelopes, it will probably be the first time in their lives that they've ever seen an envelope with 14 stamps! That envelope will catch their attention first. It will be opened first. And the contents inside will be read first. When you study direct mail, you're taught that the average response rate is 2 percent. People who send envelopes with 14 stamps enjoy a 20 percent response rate and even higher. We've heard of response rates surpassing 50 percent!

Did it take a lot of money? No. But admittedly, it did take a bit more time, a smidgeon more energy, a teeny tiny tad more information, and

THE PIZZA RESTAURANT

A pizza restaurant in Indiana used imagination to perk up its marketing strategy. Realizing the intense interest in football it printed up a two-sided circular. One side read, "half price off of any large-sized pizza at Marios" and their address. The second side said in bold print "Go Hoosiers."

It handed out the circulars at the entrance to the football stadium, and as you might imagine, after every hometown touchdown hundreds of people held up "Go Hoosiers" and thousands of people read the coupon for Marios Pizza.

a whale of a better imagination. That's how guerrillas apply their imaginations.

Some, if doing a mailing about a product from England, send their mailings to England so they can be mailing to their prospects with an English stamp. Once again, imagination wins the day for them. With hardly any of your competitors exercising such lively imaginations, it's no surprise that guerrillas win the day through direct mail. And that's why one of their key personality characteristics is their imagination.

They may not know how to draw their way out of a paper bag or write even two words that rhyme, but when it comes to the imagination to stand apart from reality, guerrilla marketers are second to none.

Trait 3: Sensitivity

A guerrilla marketer cannot plod through life thinking only of himself or herself. One of the key traits for a truly successful guerrilla is sensitivity. The guerrilla must be sensitive to

- the marketplace.
- the rural or urban environment in which the marketing is taking place.
- the economy.
- the history with his products or services, to his customers.
- his prospects.
- their families.
- the time of year.
- the competition.
- what's on his prospect's mind at the moment he is marketing.
- the time in history.

A lack of this sensitivity was demonstrated in early 2007 during the "Boston Bomb Scare," when a cartoon network owned by Turner Broadcasting promoted—or rather mis-promoted—a new TV show by placing decals in all the wrong places: near subways, bus stops, and other locales where large groups of people congregated. The decals, which had wires and duct tape attached to them, frightened many Bostonians who thought they might be bomb-related. Because two of the jet planes involved in the attack on the World Trade Center in New York in September 2001 took off from Logan Airport in Boston, it's not hard to blame those citizens of Boston for being terrified, causing traffic and public transportation throughout the city to come to a halt for hours and hours.

Had the promoters been sensitive to the mindset in Boston since 9/11, they could have chosen a different kind of promotion. Today, there is a pre-9/11 mindset and a post-9/11 mindset, calling for enhanced sensitivity, something the cartoon network promotion totally lacked. That's probably the main reason why the Turner Broadcasting Company was fined $2 million for its insensitivity.

You may not make such a horrific blunder or be fined such a substantial amount, but you could lose a lot of potential profits if you are insensitive. Guerrillas are always sensitive to the code of ethics where they operate, and to the sensibilities of the populace, being ultra-careful never to offend people or communities, never to terrify them, never to deface property, and never to be intrusive beyond the bounds of good taste.

Guerrilla marketers are sensitive to what their prospects are thinking right at the moment, to what they want, what they lack, and what they read about in the newspapers or hear on the radio. They are sensitive to the dreams of their market, striving to make these dreams come true.

As part of mass communication, marketing is part of evolution and has an obligation to be sensitive to everyone, good or bad. Without it, non-guerrillas are fighting an uphill battle.

Trait 4: Ego Strength

By *ego strength*, we don't mean having the ego to stand up to those who don't love you. It's just the opposite, it means having the ego to stand up to those who love you the most—but give you the worst marketing advice.

You craft a powerful marketing strategy, embark upon a bound-for-glory campaign, and see that all your plans are falling right into place, just as you wanted them to, and who are the first people to tire of your marketing and counsel you to change it? Usually, first it's your co-workers and then your employees, followed closely by your family, and then your best friends. "Hey, you've been doing that marketing for a long time now. I, personally, am getting pretty bored with it. Don't you think it's time to change it?" Your job: Summon up the ego to give these people a nice, warm hug, then send them on their way, knowing they know beans about your marketing.

Those people who have had their minds penetrated by your marketing three times, they're not getting bored with it. They're just learning of your existence. Those folks who have had their minds penetrated five times, the marketing momentum is just beginning with them. They last thing they want is for you to fade from view. Your current customers, they feel wonderful whenever they're exposed to your marketing because it proves that they've hitched their wagons to a winner—the kind of company that has the confidence to continue to market.

But your co-workers, family, and friends, having concentrated on your marketing from the onset, are tired of it, know it backwards and forwards, and wonder when you're going to change it. Again, they not-so-gently hint to you that perhaps you ought to drop it and move on to something else, which is another way of suggesting that you move away from your investment, move away from profitability, and move away from the momentum you've established. It takes a strong ego to look these people in the eye, give their arms a comforting squeeze, then stay with what you started. A lesser person than you, with a weaker ego, might cave in to their pressure, take their well-intended put poorly reasoned advice, and throw a marketing investment to the winds where, alas, many marketing investments end up.

> Ego strength means having the ego to stand up to those who love you the most—but give you the worst marketing advice.

If you ever thought that guerrilla marketing, especially at the beginning, is a cup of tea, this is the point where you learn that it's not for amateurs, not for insecure babies, and more like a cup of nitroglycerine that can blow up in your face if you make a crucial mistake. Lacking the ego to stand up to misinformed well-wishers is that mistake. If you're a guerrilla, you won't make it. For if you do, you're destined to repeat it each time you're at the helm of a failing business.

Trait 5: Aggressiveness

When you hear that there are 200 guerrilla marketing weapons and that more than half of them are free, if you're a guerrilla, a smile crosses your face. Somehow, your bank account lights up, and you hear the musical sounds of money jingling. Ka-ching! That's the sound of this fifth personality characteristic.

This is not to say that guerrillas are money-minded, for they're not. But it is to say that they know what it takes to obtain money. Not luck. Not a lottery. Not an inheritance, though we badmouth none of those. But aggressiveness. That's the trait we laud to the skies.

With every business utilizing just a handful of marketing weapons—three, five, ten, or even 15—the opportunity to choose from among 200 is a heady feeling. It takes an aggressive attitude to wrap your ambitions around such a lofty amount. But it's that aggressiveness that's going to separate you from the wannabe and wimpy guerrillas, if indeed, there is such a thing as a wimpy guerrilla.

We're not saying that you'll need all 200 weapons or even half of them, but you ought to be aggressive enough to want to know of their existence so you can select the ones that seem most appropriate for you. Guerrillas have a large selection. You'll find the entire list of 200 weapons waiting for you in Chapter 10.

When you learn that the average American business invested 4 percent of gross revenues in marketing in 2006, you're aggressive again. You think, "Only 4 percent? What if I invested 6 percent? Eight percent? Ten percent? You know that the average business goes out of business within five years. The last kind of company you want as a benchmark is an average business.

You're aggressive in your thinking and in your investing. Guerrillas save money not by failing to spend it but by not wasting it. Aggressiveness is your hallmark. You're among the first to use some of the new weapons of marketing. You probably have a blog. You've already begun podcasting. You've been hard at work compiling your opt-in list. This kind of aggressiveness is the sign of a leader.

Because you're aggressive in your thinking and your investing, your competitors fear you, respect you, follow you, and acknowledge your leadership. The media come to you for quotes, resulting in your getting the lion's share of free publicity. Very little goes to the lambs.

At a party or any social function, you may hide behind the foliage, speak in a soft voice, be a practicing wallflower. But when it comes to marketing, you're a lion. You're the king or queen of the entrepreneurs. You're a marketing titan—known for your visible and omnipresent marketing. As you may have heard, size doesn't matter. It's all about attitude. And yours is characterized by your aggressiveness.

> The average American business invested 4 percent of gross revenues in marketing in 2006.

Trait 6: Embracing Change

You know it and we know it: The only thing certain is change. No matter what happens in the life if your business, change is the only certainty. How you deal with change makes an enormous difference in your success—or lack of it. You can ignore change, hoping it will go away. But we're here to tell you that it won't go away. You can disdain change, detest change, or fight change. Or, you can be a guerrilla and embrace change. Be careful in how you interpret this. Change for the sake of change is not a good thing. But change for the sake of improvement is a very good thing. Don't let your negative attitude or fear of change prevent you from benefiting from the improvements.

Face up to the fact that change will continue to happen all around you, especially in marketing. How you deal with that change is what makes you a guerrilla. Get to know change on an intimate basis. Love it or hate it, but don't pay it no heed. Millions of people lost billions of dollars because they ignored the internet. Millions more lost millions more dollars because they accepted it too soon and misused or abused it.

When we urge you to embrace change, we want you to do it at the right time and for the right reasons. That takes study. That means you must pay careful attention. That means not following the crowd but following your own good instincts. Don't make the all-too-common mistake of wanting to make a change but also wanting to wait for the prices to go down. While they're taking their own sweet time going down, you could be losing a fortune while competitors are building an unsurmountable lead due to their willingness to invest at the outset while their own competitors are asleep at the wheel and saving pennies when dollars are at stake.

Embracing change is a matter of timing and knowledge, vision and guts. Guerrillas who possess this trait are rarely mired in the past and usually poised for the future. Does that describe you? We hope so.

> Millions of people lost billions of dollars because they ignored the internet.

Trait 7: Generosity

Guerrillas view their marketing as a chance to help their prospects and customers succeed at their goals. Whether that goal is earning more money, expanding a business, getting a job, losing weight, attracting a mate, or improving their golf score, they try to find ways to help them achieve their goals. Knowing that we're living smack dab in the middle of the Information Age, they are very generous in providing information.

Sometimes that information is imparted by a web site. Or it can be given in the form of an e-book, free report, consultation, seminar, or lecture. Often, instead of giving information, they give something of worth and value to their customers.

THE FULLY OCCUPIED BUILDING

A series of apartment buildings in Los Angeles had a 70 percent occupancy rate. But one of the buildings had a 100 percent occupancy rate. How did this happen? That particular building put up a sign that said, "Sign a lease . . . get free auto grooming." What the devil is auto grooming? That meant management hired a person to wash the tenants' cars once a week. The salary it paid the car washer was easily worth the difference between a 70 percent occupancy rate and a 100 percent occupancy rate. The building management simply asked itself, "What might our tenants appreciate?" The answer was simple. And their generosity in regularly performing the simple act of a weekly car wash was the difference between a highly profitable building and a so-so profitable building. No rocket science here, only common sense and a spirit of generosity.

Ask yourself, what might my prospects and customers appreciate for free? A ballpoint pen? A calendar? A pocket calendar? A refrigerator magnet? The answer need not be lavish or expensive, but merely an expression of your generosity. Flowers, plants, free samples . . . these are some of the myriad ways you can prove your generosity. You'll see that they go a long way toward bonding with your prospects and customers. They're easy to come up with if you have the spirit of generosity, if that generosity is part of your personality. Bonus for you: It's fun to give rather than receive.

Trait 8: High Energy

To practice constant acts of generosity, to consistently prove your imagination, to be aggressive in your deeds, to assess and accept change . . . all of those require a consistent display of energy. If you don't really have that energy, you can't really put your heart into all of your actions. And putting your heart into them is part of the deal.

Customers know if you're doing something because you have to and doing that same thing because you want to. They're attracted to businesses that want to serve, that want to make their customers happy.

Because being a guerrilla marketer is a full-time job, that takes energy—not sometimes energy, but all-the-time energy. A ho-hum attitude is very apparent, just as a willing attitude is easy to see. For that reason, we have seen that high-powered, highly successful guerrillas happen to be high-energy people. They bristle with energy. Everything about them is electrifying. They spread their energy throughout their workplace, even away from it. It's no surprise that they get a lot done, moving forward at all times. They are quick to greet customers, sincere in their customer relations, and ready to act without hesitation. They seem to want to take action. And the reason is that they are possessed of more than their share of energy.

> Guerrilla marketers know that by doing the work they love, they never work a day in their lives.

That helps them do the job at hand and then be ready to take on the next job. They are happy in their work, even awaken each morning looking forward to doing the work they love. That, by the way, is a key to their high energy—doing the work they love. They know that by doing the work they love, they never work a day in their lives. This love of work is always manifested by their high-energy level. That's what it takes to do all the tasks at hand, then be ready to take on more. You can sense their energy level when you see them work. Amazingly, they don't even work to demonstrate that energy. It is part of their overall personality. If you cannot make it part of yours, if high energy is not second nature to you, perhaps you should pursue a more mellow line of work. But if you can make it part of yours, you have the personality of a guerrilla who is bound for success.

Trait 9: Constant Learning

Think of a seagull. It flies endless circles in the sky, endless circles in quest of food. When it finally spots the food, the seagull lands and eats its fill. Then it rises again to the sky, only to fly in endless circles again and again. Once more, it flies in quest of food. The seagull does this because it is it's most powerful instinct.

Guerrilla marketers have an instinct that is just as powerful, just as never ending. Do you know what it is? It is the instinct for constant learning. Guerrillas learn and learn, and then learn some more. They are endlessly learning for they've learned that knowledge equates with success.

They realize that they are no longer in an age when they ought to learn all there is about a topic, but an age when they ought to be learning one thing after another. As marketing changes lightning fast, guerrillas do all in their power to continue learning about the changes in marketing. At the same time, they are learning about the peripherals of marketing: psychology, the internet, technology, and the globalization of business.

Whatever they are learning, it is a constant endeavor, just as searching for food is a constant activity of seagulls. We have never seen an exception to this observation. Each guerrilla leader that we encounter seems to be engrossed in learning new things. Truly, that is a crucial trait in all guerrillas. We hope and suspect that it is also a personality characteristic of yours.

> Guerrilla marketers have an instinct for constant learning. They've learned that knowledge equates with success.

Trait 10: Love of People

The people we have met who are running successful and profitable marketing programs know that all people are fascinating, all people are interesting, and all people—you have to dig a bit to find this one—have a lovable side. "The softer side of Sears" is how that company termed it. The idea here is that all people have a softer side.

Guerrillas look for and discover that softer side, that fascinating side, that lovable side. This interest in people is apparent in their marketing, in their marketing people, and in their treatment of clients. Guerrillas have learned that every person has a story. By being superb listeners—a key characteristic of guerrillas—they learn those stories and adjust their marketing to fit the deeper and inner core of those stories. They are also able to adjust their own stories so that they are equally fascinating, equally lovable—or at least likeable.

Guerrillas know that every person is unique, each one someone's son or daughter, father or mother, brother or sister. They honor those uniquenesses by not treating every person alike. Their honest interest in people makes them masterful communicators. And that masterful communication makes the guerrillas themselves enjoyable to hear, to listen to, to learn from.

> Guerrillas have learned that every person has a story, and adjust their marketing to fit the deeper and inner core of those stories.

People who are not interested in other people are often not interesting themselves for they tend to talk about themselves. And that's rarely someone else's main field of interest. People's prime field of interest is their own self. And they tend to listen to people who will talk about them, talk to them, care about them.

Show us a self-centered person and we'll show you someone who is not a true guerrilla marketer. Of course, everyone is not a guerrilla marketer. But all the people who run winning marketing programs certainly are.

Trait 11: The Ability to Maintain Focus

Many large and respected companies, with well-known names and abundant respect, figured that their business expertise would enable them to succeed in areas far from where they had been demonstrating their core competencies. Most of those companies, later having lost millions of dollars, realized that they were in over their heads because they allowed their corporate egos to ride herd over their common sense.

Guerrilla marketers don't make that mistake. They are skilled at their core competencies as well as skilled at maintaining their focus. They do not worship at the shrine of diversification, but instead at the shrine of excellence. Instead of going off into unchartered territories, they concentrate on adding even more excellence to their current endeavors. They strive to do what they've always been doing, only doing it better than they have before.

Technology and experience enable them to succeed at that goal. Those factors enable them to keep their focus while making it even more acute. Mind you, it's not easy to maintain your focus. In today's world, distractions abound. Side tracks woo many a leader from his or her chosen path. Almost always, trouble lurks at the end of those roads.

Maintaining your focus sounds easy but is hard. This does not mean that you should resist change but that you should accept it if it helps to keep you on track, on target, and on the money. But if it causes you to veer from your target and diffuse your focus, steer clear of it. We have seen many train wrecks caused by following tracks that led off the edge of the cliff.

We have also seen many century-old companies earning more than ever because they were able to resist the temptation of novelty and corporate confusion while staying the course. A word of warning to start-up businesses: You will be tempted often to go for the gold at the expense of your focus. We have nothing to say against gold and only four golden words to say about focus: Maintain it or else.

> Guerrilla marketers are skilled at their core competencies as well as skilled at maintaining their focus. They do not worship at the shrine of diversification, but instead at the shrine of excellence.

Trait 12: Taking Action

In seminars, presentations, and assorted trainings we have done around the world, we have learned by simple before-and-after observation that people have one-way brains or two-way brains. People with one-way brains read books, attend seminars, take copious notes during presentations, pay rapt attention during trainings, study the internet, learn from mentors, listen to CDs, watch DVDs, take courses, participate in tele-seminars, and learn as much as is humanly possible. The information they absorb is assimilated, memorized, and understood. But it remains within them, which is no place for important information to reside.

People with two-way brains absorb the same information, but then they take action on it. They know darned well that guerrilla marketing is not a spectator sport. They realize that information not acted upon is wasted information. They act on the advice they are given. They breathe life into the concepts they have learned. They experiment. They know that action is the name of the game to guerrillas. Because they have two-way brains, they do something about what they have learned.

> Guerrilla marketing is not a spectator sport.

While others may learn by hearing, guerrillas learn by doing. They are a very hands-on group of people. That laying on of the hands is one of their many secrets of success. If your personality does not include the proclivity to take action, change that aspect of your personality.

We are not writing this book as an academic exercise, but as a method for you to learn exactly what you must do with guerrilla marketing. The key word in that sentence is "do."

PERSONALITY CHARACTERISTICS OF GUERRILLAS

1. Patience
2. Imagination
3. Sensitivity
4. Ego strength
5. Aggressiveness
6. Embraces change
7. Generosity
8. Energetic
9. Constant learning
10. People person
11. Maintains focus
12. Takes action

3

GUERRILLA MARKETING YOURSELF

Guerrilla marketers know that success involves not only choosing the right guerrilla marketing weapons, but also using them as effectively as possible. Appearance plays a major role in the effectiveness of your guerrilla marketing program. You must always be "on," projecting yourself in as favorable a way as possible.

Graphic design plays a major role in determining the identity you project in your marketing materials. From the appearance of your ads, brochures, business cards, newsletters, presentation visuals, and web site, prospects will make instant decisions about your credibility and ability to satisfy their needs. Accordingly, it's vital that you become aware of some of the subtle influences that can promote or hinder the identity you project to clients and prospects. After analyzing your current marketing materials, you may want to redo some of them in order to project a fine-tuned and positive identity.

This chapter also focuses on the identity you project to clients and prospects who meet you face-to-face.

Are you best described as neat and clean or casual? Is it possible to figure out what you had for breakfast yesterday from your shirt? Do you need a haircut? Appearance plays a major role in determining the identity you project in print, in person, and online.

> Appearance plays a major role in the effectiveness of your guerrilla marketing program.

Describing Your Business to Your Prospects

You can have the best product or service in the world, but many potential clients won't be interested in your professional services unless you can convince them in a very personal way. There are two steps you should consider to define your marketing message. Let's take a short quiz to see how well you accomplish this.

Step 1

Describe your business in ten seconds or less, using seven words or less. The goal here is to create focus and to arouse curiosity.

Example 1: "We coach businesses to increase their profits."

Example 2: "We sell computers at the lowest prices."

How would you describe your business in seven words or less?

_____

Step 2

After engaging a person's interest, you can describe your business in more detail, using an interactive conversational style. Be sure to address the benefits of your service and your competitive advantage. Use words that inspire.

How would you describe your business in more detail?

_____

Presenting Yourself

Guerrilla marketers realize that their clients and customers judge their competence at every point of contact. So guerrilla marketers pay constant attention to the way they present themselves and strive for constant improvement. There are two categories of presentations: *time-lapse* and *realtime*.

Time-Lapse Presentations

Time-lapse presentations are characterized by a delay between the time the guerrilla marketer prepares his or her message and the time clients or prospects read it. The message may be prepared hours, days, weeks, or months ahead of time. As a result, time-lapse presentations are one-way communications: They cannot be changed on the fly because they can't observe every reader's reaction.

This delay between creation and reading places a great burden on the appearance or formatting of the guerrilla's message. The entire message must compensate for the facial expressions, gestures, and vocal intonations that readers can't see but use to judge messages that are delivered face to face. As a result, time-lapse communications are extremely detail intensive. Formatting errors, such as the random placement of text and graphics on a page, the inconsistent use of color and type, or constantly changing typeface and type size undermines the message. Likewise, editing problems like transposed words or spelling errors destroy the identity of competence and professionalism guerrilla marketers strive to project at every point of contact.

There are three categories of time-lapse communications:

> Time-lapse presentations are characterized by a delay between the time the guerrilla marketer prepares his or her message and the time clients or prospects read it.

1. *Print.* Ads, brochures, business cards, newsletters, proposals, and reports.
2. *Online.* Your web site.
3. *E-mail.* Including e-mail sent to clients as well as postings to online forums.

We discuss web sites and e-mail in more detail in a later chapter.

> Real-time presentations are two-way communications.

Real-Time Communications

Real-time presentations are two-way communications. Guerrillas not only enhance their message with gestures by varying their tone of voice, but also drive home their point by maintaining eye contact and occasionally smiling. Guerrillas can alter their real-time presentation by observing their client's reaction to their words. They can read their client's body language and react accordingly.

There are two types of real-time presentations:

1. *Telephone.* Using incoming or outgoing calls to communicate with clients.
2. *Face-to-face.* One-to-one or group presentations in a conference room or at a speaker's podium.

> *"You only have one chance
> to make a good first impression."*

You Are Always On-Stage

Whether you know it or not, you're marketing yourself every day. And to *lots of people!* You're marketing yourself to make a sale, warm up a relationship, get a job, get connected, and get something you deserve. You're always sending messages about yourself—either intentionally or unintentionally.

Intention

Guerrillas control the messages that they send—*it's all about intention!* Non-guerrillas send unintentional messages, even if those messages sabotage their overall goals in life. They want to close a sale for a consulting contract, but their inability to make eye contact or the mumbled message they leave on an answering machine turns off the prospect.

Guerrillas send no unintentional messages. Unintentional messages erect an insurmountable barrier. Your job: Be sure there is no barrier. There are really two people within you—your accidental self and your intentional self. Most people are able to conduct about 95 percent of their lives by intent. But that's not enough. It's the other 5 percent that can get you in trouble—or in clover. We're not talking phoniness here. The idea is for you to be who you are and not who you aren't—to be aware of what you're doing, aware of whether or not your actions communicate ideas that will help you get what you deserve.

Take a personal inventory. *How do you send messages and market yourself right now?*

- Your appearance
- You also market with your eye contact
- Body language
- Your habits
- Your speech patterns
- Your letters, e-mail, web site, notes, faxes, brochures, and other printed material
- Your attitude
- Your ethics

> There are really two people within you—your accidental self and your intentional self.

How People Judge You

Again, you may not be aware of it, but people are constantly judging and assessing you by noticing many things about you. You must be sure the messages of your marketing don't fight your dreams.

> You must be sure the messages of your marketing don't fight your dreams.

TRAITS PEOPLE USE TO MAKE DECISIONS ABOUT YOU

- Clothing
- Hair
- Weight
- Height
- Jewelry
- Facial hair
- Makeup
- Business card
- Laugh
- Glasses
- Title
- Neatness
- Smell
- Teeth
- Smile
- What you carry
- Eye contact
- Gait
- Posture
- Tone of voice
- Handwriting
- Spelling
- Hat
- Thoughtfulness
- Car
- Office
- Home
- Nervous habits
- Handshake
- Stationery
- Availability
- Writing ability
- Phone use
- Enthusiasm
- Energy level
- Comfort online

You should be fully aware of your intentional marketing and invest time, energy, and imagination in it, not to mention money. But you may be undermining that investment if you're not paying attention to things that matter to others even more than what you say:

- Keeping promises
- Punctuality
- Honesty
- Demeanor

- Respect
- Gratitude
- Sincerity
- Feedback
- Initiative
- Reliability
- Passion—or the absence of it
- How well you listen to them

> *"Big-heartedness is the most essential*
> *virtue on the spiritual journey."*
>
> —MATTHEW FOX

Because you have so many kinds of exposure to your business, you'll benefit from learning the key tips for looking good in print, sounding good on the radio, and appearing good in person.

Looking Good in Print
Tips and Techniques for Ads, Brochures, Business Cards, Memos, Newsletters, and Proposals

The quality of your print communications plays a major role in the way clients and prospects judge your competence and professionalism. Perception equals reality. If your print communications project a haphazard, devil-may-care identity, that's the way you will be judged—regardless of your actual competence and professionalism. Here are eight ideas to help you present yourself more professionally in print.

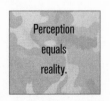

Perception
equals
reality.

1. *Strive for consistency.* Minimize change. Use the same typeface and color choices throughout all of your print communications. Choose a core set of typefaces and a consistent color palette of

a limited number of colors that work well together. Faithfully use these throughout all of your print communications.

2. *Add white space.* Avoid cramped pages. Use white space—the absence of text or graphics to make your publications project a distinct and easy to read identity. Use white space in the margins of your publications to focus your reader's eyes on your message as well as make it easy for readers to hold your brochure or newsletter without their thumbs obscuring some of the words.

3. *Chunk content.* Insert frequent subheads to break long articles into a series of easier-to-read mini-articles. Each subhead advertises the paragraphs that follow and provides an additional entry point into your text.

4. *Align elements.* Avoid visuals such as charts, illustrations, or photographs that appear seemingly "dropped in" to your pages. Align the borders of your photographs with each other or the underlying column structure that organizes your pages.

5. *Exercise restraint.* Eliminate unnecessary graphic elements. Today's desktop publishing software makes it too easy to add unnecessary page borders, vertical lines between columns, or decorative clipart. Instead, try to make as few "marks" on the page as possible. Just as your writing gains strength by eliminating unnecessary words, your correspondence, brochures, and newsletters will project a more professional image if there is a good reason for every graphic element on the page.

6. *Use upper-case type with restraint.* Headlines and subheads set entirely in upper case type such as all capital letters occupy more space and are significantly harder to read than headlines and subheads set in lower case type.

7. *Never underline.* Underlining instantly projects an amateurish, typewriter-like image. Underlined words are significantly harder to read than the same words set in bold or italics. The

only time underlined words should appear in your print publications is to indicate web site addresses and e-mail addresses.

8. *Sweat the details.* Avoid visual distractions such as awkward sentence spacing when two spaces are inserted after periods. Avoid widows and orphans—subheads or single lines of text beginning new paragraphs isolated at the bottom of a page or sentence fragments isolated by themselves at the top of a column or page. Make sure that your software has inserted the proper punctuation, such as curved open and closed quotation marks and apostrophes, rather than straight up and down foot and inch marks.

Successful guerrilla marketers recognize that their message is judged as much by its appearance as by its content. Don't reserve these tips for formal publications like brochures and newsletters, printed in color in large numbers by commercial printers. Your everyday correspondence, especially your proposals and reports, deserve as much attention to presentation detail as your formal, printed brochures and newsletters.

THE HIGH-POWERED WEAPON IN YOUR OFFICE

There will rarely be as intimate a moment as those you spend on the phone with customers and prospects. People will be judging you by your voice and the content of your words.

If you want to gain the maximum respect, lower your voice. It will help you sound more credible, more trustworthy, more knowledgeable. At the same time, speak a bit slower. This helps you sound less frantic, more patient, more able to solve problems.

Use the person's name or name of his or her business. If you smile while you're on the phone, that smile comes through into the other person's ears, then brain. With all this advice, be sure you don't fail to get to the point—within the first 30 seconds of your call. Try to tell the person you're calling about something they didn't know before. Along with your smile, let your passion and enthusiasm show through. But don't be silly about it. Guerrillas never cross the silly line.

Sounding Good on the Phone

Before dialing the phone, savvy telemarketers ask themselves questions like:

- What do I know about the prospect?
- What do I *need to know* in order for the prospect to take the action desired?
- What information might be obtained from a database or screener?
- What do I say if voice-mail technology answers the call?
- What will my opening statement be?
- What questions will I ask?
- How will I end the call (no matter what happens)?

Guerrilla marketers ask themselves similar questions, and rehearse their telephone techniques.

Voice Training

No matter who does the calling, proper voice training is a good idea. Talk clearly. Use short sentences. Talk loud enough but not directly into the mouthpiece. Talking across the mouthpiece gives the most effective voice transmission. Your voice should project authority and warmth while instilling trust. Your message should be stated as concisely as possible.

> Guerrillas are in full control of their telemarketing and do not recite awkward speeches to their prospects.

Analyze Yourself

Notice how your friends, and probably even you, assume different voice personalities when speaking on the phone. This is subtle, but it's there. Try to eliminate that telephone personality and bring out your most conversational qualities by actually practicing on the phone—talking to a tape recorder or to a friend.

Script or Not to Script?

Whatever you do, don't read from a script. However, research shows that it's always a good idea to *memorize* a script, changing any words that feel awkward or uncomfortable. The script must be so well memorized that the words sound as though you know them by heart—as natural as the Pledge of Allegiance.

Don't use words that feel strange to say. Find words and phrases that come naturally to you. Leave time for the person on the other end to respond. Guerrillas are in full control of their telemarketing and do not recite awkward speeches to their prospects. Doing so is bad business—more personal than a computer pitch, but still not worth doing if not done right.

Studies in various industries consistently show that a memorized telemarketing presentation always produces better results than the same presentation from an outline. You may think it's better to let the caller use his or her own words, but few callers have the ability to summon the right ones.

Gone are the days when it was recommended that callers use an outline, or thought-flow. Still, the more naturally conversant you sound, the more sales you'll make—and that takes practice. Naturally, much of what you say will be in response to what the person being called says, but the best telemarketers are in full control of the call. They stay in control by asking questions, responding to the answers, then asking more questions, directing the conversation toward the customers getting what they need and a sale being made.

If you are still more comfortable using an outline to structure your phone presentations, heed the following guidelines:

> Studies in various industries consistently show that a memorized telemarketing presentation always produces better results than the same presentation from an outline.

- If the outline is longer than one page, there is probably too much in it and you should try to streamline it.
- An outline does create a structure for your thoughts and ideas, and also helps keep the call on track when the person at the other end redirects it.
- Even if you do work from an outline, it's still a good idea to write a script of a phone call.

Working with a Script

Once you have written the script, you should do three things with it:

1. *Record it.* See what it sounds like. After all, you'll be using "ear" words that are heard, rather than "eye" words that are seen. There's a big, big difference.
2. *Conversational.* Make sure the recorded script sounds like a conversation and not like an ad. Leave room for the person being called to talk.

WORDS CALLERS UNCONSCIOUSLY LOVE TO HEAR

• Profits	• Morale
• Sales	• Motivation
• Dollars	• Output
• Revenues	• Attitude
• Income	• Image
• Cash flow	• Victories
• Savings	• Market share
• Time	• Competitive edge
• Productivity	

3. *Rephrase not repeat.* Make it a point not to restate the script but to rephrase it. State the same selling points. Present them in the same order. But use words with which you are comfortable.

Your telephone planning should be able to accommodate several situations. After all, if your prospect decides to buy just after you've started, you should be prepared to close the sale and end the conversation.

Role Playing

If you're going to do a good amount of telephone marketing, engage in role-playing, with you as the customer and a friend or associate as you. Then switch roles. Role-playing gives you a lot of insight into your offering and your message. Keep doing this until you are completely satisfied with your presentation.

> Asking questions is the best way to prepare a successful presentation.

Planning Your Presentation

Asking questions is the best way to prepare a successful presentation. Get in the habit of using the following worksheet (Figure 4.1) to plan your presentations.

FIGURE 4.1: **Presentation Worksheet**

Section 1. Purpose

1. What is your message? _____

_____

2. What does the client want from you? _____

_____

FIGURE 4.1: **Presentation Worksheet,** continued

3. What is your desired outcome from the presentation? _____

    _____

4. What are the client's next steps or actions after the presentation? _____

    _____

5. What information do you need to obtain during the presentation? _____

    _____

Section 2. Resources

1. How much time do you have? _____

    _____

2. Who will be attending? _____

    _____

Section 3. Content

1. What three things do you want your audience to remember? _____

    _____

    _____

2. What are your three P's (purpose, process, and payoff) for the presentation? ____

    _____

    _____

3. What statistics are relevant for this presentation? _____

    _____

FIGURE 4.1: **Presentation Worksheet,** continued

4.   What gifts can you use in your presentation? _____

_____

5.   What new research or information can you use in this presentation? _____

_____

6.   What questions can you ask? _____

_____

7.   What creative openers can you use to engage the audience? _____

_____

8.   How can you stretch yourself during this presentation? _____

_____

9.   What exercises can you do to get the point across? _____

_____

10. How will you end or summarize your presentation? _____

_____

5

MARKETING FACE TO FACE

You can be certain that the first commerce was transacted face to face, one caveman to another. That method continues on, mostly in the form of selling, which is a blessing to some people who love to do it and a curse to others who find the instinct absent from their DNA.

Advice to a guerrilla who faces a lifetime of face-to-face selling: Learn to love it by learning about sales and by learning more about your product or service. The more you know about these things, the more passionate you can be when get to do them or to sell them. As in so many parts of our life on earth, passion rules the roost and fuels the fires.

Once you learn to excel at face-to-face selling, you'll find yourself considering selling to more than one person, such as in a seminar, in a webinar, or on a teleconference. As hot and sexy as computers may be, teleconferences—disdaining the use of visuals, and relying on the good old telephone—are being held in record numbers.

The guerrilla feels equally comfortable speaking directly to a person while looking into that person's eyes, or speaking to a 1,000 people while looking into a TV camera lens. Never forget that marketing is just a fancy word that means selling.

Getting Them to Look You in the Eye and Buy

You need to see yourself as others see you. The following tips, excerpted from Jay Conrad Levinson's *Guerrilla Marketing, 4th Edition* (Houghton Mifflin, 2007) should help. Use them to help you evaluate and develop rapport, give dynamic presentations, and most of all, close the sale.

Contact

The tone of your meeting is established early. Here are some ways you can create a positive first impression.

- *Greet your prospect warmly and sincerely*, using eye contact.
- *Allow your prospect some time to get acclimated* to being with you, some time to talk. Don't come on too strong. But don't waste your prospect's time, either.
- *Engage in casual conversation at first*—especially about anything pertinent to your prospect. Make it friendly and not one-sided. Be a good listener. But, let the prospect know that your time is precious. You are there to sell, not to talk.
- *Ask relevant questions*. Listen carefully to the answers.
- *Qualify the prospect*. Determine whether or not this is the specific person to whom you should be talking, the person with the authority to give you the go-ahead, to buy.
- *Learn something about the person to whom your contact is directed* so that he or she will feel like a person rather than a prospect.

Make your prospect like you, for people enjoy doing business with people they like. The best possible thing you can do is to make your prospect feel unique—proving that you recognize his or her individuality and needs.

- *Be brief, friendly, outgoing, and truly inquisitive.* But, be yourself.
- *If you're in a retail environment,* one of the best questions to initiate healthy contact is "Mind if I ask what brings you into our store today?"
- *Don't think of yourself as a salesperson but as a partner to your prospect.* This healthy mindset improves both your perspective and your chances of closing. Realize that you have an opportunity to educate your prospects to succeed at whatever they wish to succeed at. As soon as possible, learn what it is that your prospect wishes to succeed at, and then show how what you are selling can make that success achievable.
- *Important elements of your contact are your smile, your attire, your posture, and your willingness to listen and look directly into the prospect's eyes.* Your nonverbal communication is as important as your verbal communication. The impression you make will come as much from what you don't say as from what you do say.

Your Presentation

When making your presentation, keep in mind that you are not talking by accident. You are there because of intent on your part. If your prospect is still with you, there is intent on his or her part, too. And the intent is to buy.

Either you will buy a story about why a sale cannot be made, or your prospect will buy what you're selling. It truly is up to you. And don't forget: People do enjoy being sold to. They do not like being pressured. They do like being *persuaded* by honest enthusiasm to buy.

The following are some tips to make your presentations flow smoothly and some ways to evaluate your technique.

- *List all the benefits of doing business with you, one by one.* The more benefits a prospect knows about, the more likely a prospect will buy. When compiling your list of benefits, invite your employees and at least one customer. Customers are tuned in to benefits you offer that you may take for granted.
- *Emphasize the unique advantages of buying from you.* You should be able to rattle these off with the same aplomb you can state your own name and address. It is upon these competitive advantages that you should be basing your marketing. Don't knock your competition whatever you do.
- *Stress the advantages of your type of offering, then of your specific offering,* especially if your prospect has no experience with what you are selling. If you're selling security devices, talk of the value of owning them, then of the value of owning yours.
- *Tailor your presentation.* Do your homework and find out what there is to know about your contact. Then take that information and customize it into your presentation.
- *Mention the acceptance of your products or services by others—especially people in their community.* People do not like to be pioneers. People know darned well that pioneers get arrows in the back of their necks. If you can mention names and be specific, by all means do so. The more specific you are, the more closes you'll make. But don't be tedious. You can't bore a prospect into buying.
- *Know enough about your prospect so you can present your product or service from his or her point of view.* This ability will increase your number of closes dramatically. Emphasize what all of your product or service benefits can do for your prospect, not what they can do for the general population.
- *Keep an eagle eye on your prospect's eyes, teeth, and hands.* If the prospect is looking around, rather than at you, you've got to say something to regain attention. If your prospect is not smiling, you are being too serious. Say something to earn a smile.

Best of all, smile yourself. That will get your prospect to smile. If your prospect is wringing his or her hands, your prospect is bored. Say something to ease the boredom and spark more interest.

- *So show as much as you can: photos, drawings, a circular, a product, your sales video, anything.* A sales point made to the eye is 78 percent more effective than one made to the ear. Just be sure it relates to your presentation.

- *Sell the benefit along with the feature.* If the feature is solar power, for instance, the benefit is economy. If the feature is new computer software, the benefit is probably speed, power, or profitability.

- *Mention your past successes*, so the prospect will feel that the key to success is in your hands and there is little chance of a ripoff.

- *Be proud.* Take pride in your prices, benefits, and offering. Convey your pride with facial expressions, tone of voice, and selection of words. Feel the pride and let it come shining through.

- *Remain convinced that your prospect will buy from you throughout your presentation.* This optimism will be sensed by the prospect and can positively affect the close.

There are 250,000 commonly used words in the English language; there are 600,000 nonverbal methods of communications: stance, facial expression, hand gestures, eyebrow position and 599,996 others. Learn them and utilize them. They're completely free, a perfect example of pure guerrilla marketing. No cost, high payoff.

> There are 250,000 commonly used words in the English language; there are 600,000 nonverbal methods of communications: stance, facial expression, hand gestures, eyebrow position, and 599,996 others.

Close

Despite the importance we have attached to the contact and the presentation, we still reiterate that all the marbles are in the close. Effective salespeople and canvassers are effective closers.

Aim to be a dynamite closer and your income will reflect this. To close effectively, try to close immediately, rather than in a week or so.

Review the tips here and note how frequently you utilize the techniques.

- *Always assume that your prospective customer is going to do what you want*, so you can close with a leading question such as, "Will it be better for you to take delivery this week or next week?" "Do you want it in gray or brown?"
- *Summarize your main points and confidently end with a closing line* such as, "Everything seems to be in order. Why don't I just write up your order now?"
- *Ask the customer to make some kind of decision, and then close on it.* Typical points that must be agreed upon are delivery date, size of order, and method of payment. A good closing would be: "I can perform this service for you tomorrow, the 8th, or the 15th. The 8th would be best for me. Which would be best for you?"

  Begin to attempt the close as soon as possible by easing your prospect into it. If that time doesn't work, try again, then again. Continue trying. If you don't, your prospect will spend his or her hard-earned money elsewhere—and with someone else. Count on that. Remember: People like to be sold to and need to have the deal closed. They won't make the close themselves. So *you are performing a service* when you sell and close.

  Always be on the alert for signs that the time is right to close. The prospect will hardly ever tell you when the time has come. You must look for hints in the prospect's words and actions. A mere shifting of weight from one foot to another may be a signal to close.

- *Try to give your prospect a good reason to close immediately.* It may be that you won't be back in the neighborhood for a long time, the prospect will wish to use your product or service as soon as possible, prices are expected to rise, or you have the time and the inventory now but might not later.
- *Let your prospect know of the success of your product or service* with people like the prospect, with people recently, or with people in

the community—people with whom the prospect can easily relate.

- *Be specific with names, dates, costs, times, and benefits.* Evasiveness in any area works against you.

- *If the prospect likes what you say but won't close now, ask, "Why wait?"* The prospect may then voice an objection. And you may close by saying, "That's great, and I understand." Then you can solve the objection and close on it. In fact, one of the easiest ways to close is to search for an objection, then solve the problem, and close on it.

   If you have not yet completed your presentation but feel the time may be right to close, attempt to close on the most important sales point you have yet to state. Always remember that a person knows what you want him or her to do, that there is a reason for your meeting, that your offering does have merit, and that at that moment, your prospect has your offering on his or her mind. Just knowing all these things will make it easier for you to close. When a prospect says, "Let me think it over," that means "no."

- *If you do not close after your presentation, chances are you have lost the sale.* Few prospects have the guts to tell you they will definitely not buy from you. They search for excuses. So do everything you can to move them into a position where they will buy from you. If you don't, a better salesperson will.

- *Tie the close in with the contact.* Try to close on a personal note. Something like, "I think you'll feel more secure now with this new security system, and that's important. Shall I have it installed tomorrow or the next day?"

Guerrilla marketing involves all aspects of the way you present yourself to clients, customers, and prospects. The design of your print and online communications, the appearance and readability of your e-mail messages, the way you respond to telephone calls, and your appearance all influence your market's perception of your competence and professionalism.

We have barely scratched the surface of what "appropriate behavior" is for guerrilla marketers. Consistently following these suggestions will take you a long way toward projecting a competent, professional identity and being the type of person prospects, customers, and clients want to be around.

> It costs guerrilla marketers six times more to sell something to a prospect than to sell that same thing to a customer.

What's a Customer Worth?

Guerrillas strive for and savor long-term relationships with their customers. They well know the myriad of benefits of long-lasting connections and do all in their power to establish and nourish them. They're well aware that it costs them six times more to sell something to a prospect than to sell that same thing to a customer. It's one thing, however, to know the value of a long-term relationship, and it's something entirely different to *engage in activities* that spawn such delicious connections.

Take a minute to determine "What's the value of each of your customers over his or her lifetime?" Write down the answer, and post it over your desk and share it with your employees.

FEDEX

Federal Express is a company that focuses on the value of a customer. If a mid-sized company sends 30 packages a week at $25 each, that's $750 a week, or $18,750 a year. If a customer gets angry over a $25 shipment and switches her business to a competitor, Federal Express loses thousands and thousands of dollars. That's why every Federal Express supervisor is authorized to grant a $100 refund on the spot, no questions asked, for any delayed shipments. A $100 refund is a small price to pay to keep an $18,750 a year customer.

Why is this statistic so important? Because the value of your customers helps you determine how much you might be willing to spend to acquire a new customer. And, just as important, it forces you to realize *how much it costs you to lose a customer once you've got him or her.* Use Figure 5.1 to help you figure our a customer's value.

FIGURE 5.1: **The Value of a Customer Worksheet**

1. If you continue to provide good service and quality, how long will the customer patronize your business? _____

   _____

2. How much money will this customer spend on your products or services in a year? _____

   _____

3. Multiply the amount of money spent in a year by the length of time this customer purchases your goods and/or services.

   $_____

4. The result is the lifetime value of this customer.

   $_____

This number should be engraved on your forehead, and you should share it with all your employees. It will help you focus on the critical elements of building your business.

Relationships for Guerrilla Marketers
No Person—and No Business—Is an Island

The chemistry of a long-term relationship is as complex as the chemistry of a long-term and happy marriage. The starting point is a commitment to the happiness of someone else. The next point is a goal not of customer satisfaction, because that's relatively simple and common, but of *customer bliss*—exceeding the expectations of customers, *giving more* than they anticipated, and *caring more* than they're used to sellers caring.

To do this, you've got to *learn about them*. You learn first by listening to them, then by asking more questions and listening carefully once again. Guerrillas often ask those questions on their web sites or with specially prepared customer questionnaires, which solicit personal information. By knowing the personal likes and dislikes of your customers you can render personalized service—clipping articles of interest to special customers or recognizing their achievements and the achievements of their families or businesses.

Some additional ways to use a personal touch when dealing with customers are:

- Handwritten notes on mailings make the customers feel singled out.
- Phone calls that are not part of a telemarketing campaign accomplish the same.
- Using the customers' names, talking with them on nonbusiness topics.
- Alerting them to special new products or services you have available.
- Responding instantly to their calls, e-mails, faxes, and letters.

All those seemingly insignificant actions act as beneficial catalysts in the chemistry of a healthy buyer-seller relationship. The more details you know of your customers' lives and businesses, the more empowered you are to mention those details, making each customer feel unique and special rather than part of a large demographic group.

Guerrillas have the insight to know that there's an extraordinary chemistry that exists in long-term relationships. It doesn't happen automatically. It doesn't happen instantly. But when it does happen, the business owner is as delighted as the customer. Figure 5.2 helps you rate your relationship building.

FIGURE 5.2: **Are You an Effective Relationship Builder?**

Take your relationship inventory. Read each statement and rate yourself on a scale of from 1 to 10 (1 = never, 10 = always).

Answer every question not only from your own perspective, but as a client or customer would answer for you.

		Score
1.	I strike up conversations with strangers and share my business frequently with them.	
2.	My marketing plan includes attending regular networking events.	
3.	I remember personal details about people and share them at an appropriate moment to let them know I care about them.	
4.	My clients are a great source of referrals, which I tap on a regular basis.	
5.	I follow-up with potential clients within 48 hours.	
6.	I believe that everyone is a potential client.	
7.	When I'm out and about, I look and act professional.	
8.	I'm fun to be around. People love to talk to me.	

FIGURE 5.2: **Are You an Effective Relationship Builder?,** continued

	Score
9. My community can count on me to be there. I often participate in community programs and frequently volunteer.	
10. I feel confident in myself.	
11. I remember to acknowledge people's strengths.	
12. I enjoy speaking in front of groups.	
13. I sell my services to a person, not another client or a corporation.	
14. People are extraordinary. I look for the good in all people.	
15. My business is oriented to giving. I often provide free consultations, tips, gifts, and information.	
16. I ask my friends to introduce me to potential clients.	
17. People contribute to me on a regular basis.	
18. I see myself as a resource for others.	
19. My networking and relationship-building skills have produced many clients over the last six months.	

6

THE TOP TEN ATTRIBUTES OF A GUERRILLA MARKETER

We hope you're not misled by our top ten choices here. If we had more time, we could make a case for 200 choices. Our fear is that you'll become so focused on these ten that you won't aim your gray matter at other attributes. So say after us, "I (state your name) promise to open my mind to more than merely the top ten attributes, and will consider them a path more than a final destination. That crucial point I acknowledge and swear."

Attribute 1: Name

While beginning your march forward into your first guerrilla marketing venture, be extra careful not to stumble with your first step—the selection of a name. Many companies do, which is why so many have misguided and misleading names. To prevent yours from faltering at the outset, there are be-sures to help you do a bang-up job:

- *Be sure it breaks the rules.* Names that easily fit in with the crowd are names that are easily forgotten. Your name should command attention right at the start, then maintain that attention throughout the life of your business. If it reminds you of any of your competitors' names, drop it before you help them.

- *Be sure it forces your competitors to wince.* Your registered brand name is something they can't take away from you, so be sure it makes them feel uncomfortable. It if makes them squirm and they can't copy it, you've done a good job in the naming department.

- *Be sure it is simple to pronounce and spell.* Hah! We should talk with a name like "guerrilla." Eighty percent of people who visit our web site spell it wrong, forcing us to buy up all the misspellings and to name our web site www.gmarketing.com. Hey, do as we say, but don't always do as we do, especially in the easy-to-spell department.

- *Be sure it tells a story or makes a promise.* Truly good names are like teeny-tiny poems, like "Lean Cusine." Each letter, each word, each sound should work with the others to deliver a message. The right name will actually attract customers to your business. That's only one of the reasons why it is such a potent marketing tool.

- *Be sure it suggests a feature or a benefit.* Think of the most powerful benefit that you offer, then create a name around it. When customers see your name, they will be clear about what you offer to them. How many names fail to do that? Most of them. Don't let your name be one of them.

- *Be sure you take a chance with your name.* Putting it into the comfort zone is like putting it into the invisible zone. Make people sit up and take notice the moment they see or hear your name.

Truly good names are like teeny-tiny poems, like "Lean Cusine."

If they read it, then forget it, you didn't take a chance. Guts and courage are part of the name game.

- *Be sure you don't name yourself into a corner.* Don't call yourself Pied Piper Children's Furniture if there's a chance you might become a purveyor of general furniture as well. Don't be Blake and Austin's Repair Shop if Blake and Austin might not be partners for life. Don't let your name prohibit you from expanding, diversifying, or growing. Name changes are like having teeth pulled, only more painful.

The keys to bad names are those that are tough to pronounce, limit your business, exaggerate, or might remind folks of another company, and are spelled "guerrilla" because they're a bear, not a gorilla, to spell. You know our feelings about those.

If you're going to use the Yellow Pages, remember that names appearing first on a list get the majority of calls. So start your name with an A or better still, AA or even better, AAA. If you have a short name, you can use larger letters in your ad. A large name looks more impressive in marketing than a small name.

Your name can work for you or against you, or just sit there and not work at all. As you get only one chance to make a first impression, you also get only one chance to name your company at the outset. Want to venture a wild guess as to which part of your business gets the most use by the most people? You got it—your name.

> The keys to bad names are those that are tough to pronounce, limit your business, exaggerate, or might remind folks of another company.

Attribute 2: Branding

Fish gotta swim, birds gotta fly, guerrillas gotta brand or they'll be lost in the fray. It's your branding that's going to help people trust you. That's what's going to break down the barrier between never-heard-of-you and can't-wait-till-I-talk-with-you. Branding reassures people that they aren't the first lemmings off the cliff.

Your product or service can be more than a product or service. It can be a brand-name product or a brand-name service. That means

We were driving to an ad agency presentation and spoke excitedly about the presentation we were about to make. The cab driver turned his head to say "you guys really believe that advertising stuff works?" He was definitely not an ideal customer. Or was he? "It doesn't work for me." He added " I never would buy a product because of advertising. Never have. Never will." One of our people asked him, " What kind of toothpaste do you use?" "Oh, I use Gleam," he said, "But it has nothing to do with the advertising. It's because I drive a cab and I can't brush after every meal." Such is the power of branding. To him. To you. To us.

people will have faith in you more than others and will even pay more money to purchase what you've got for sale. Some brands are so embraced by people that they sport tattoos attesting to their loyalty. Harley-Davidson is a case in point. And we use the word point intentionally, feeling only a tinge of guilt.

It should be apparent that you probably can't brand yourself overnight. Like most great marketing, it takes time. And commitment. And consistency. Without consistency, there can be no brand. It's the repetitive exposure that ingrains a brand in people's unconscious minds, ready to spring into action when they're in a buying situation.

> Without consistency, there can be no brand. It's the repetitive exposure that ingrains a brand in people's unconscious minds.

Branding seems to favor the visual depiction, such as Tony the Tiger or the golden arches, but it also seems to favor the verbal form, such as Coca-Cola or Mmmm . . . Mmmm . . . Good. The idea is to have any kind of a repeatable, simple, understandable, venerable brand.

If you want to go for the gold, realize that the gold follows the people who have earned brand name awareness. Get it in the print media, the electronic media, the internet, word-of-mouse, billboards, wherever you can. But get it as soon as you can. Waiting is the opposite of branding.

Why Branding Is Important

Marketers use branding to develop the perception, creating the impression that a brand has certain qualities or characteristics that make it special or unique. The following identifies some of those perceptions and their importance.

- In a complex world, people gravitate towards brand names. The more complicated the world, the greater the power of a brand.

- The more complicated the world gets, the more comforting the familiar will seem, and the better it will get for brands.

- The number-one reason that people patronize a business is because of confidence in that business. A brand name fosters confidence.

- The *Harvard Business Review* says that it's impossible to succeed in the 21st century unless you have a brand name.

- Brands are the rock stars of commerce and have loyal fans.

- The future of marketing belongs to the businesses who have the strongest brand name awareness.

- To create a brand, all you need is clear vision, a sense of purpose, genius, faith, and perseverance.

- Great brands do not happen overnight. The three most important things you need to establish a brand are time, consistency, and behavior in keeping with that brand.

- A brand includes the overall purchase experience enjoyed by the customer.

- A brand is a living entity—and it is enriched or undermined cumulatively over time, the product of a thousand small gestures.

- If Coca-Cola's assets were destroyed overnight, the next day the owner of the name could walk into a bank and get a loan to rebuild everything. Such is the immense power of a brand.

- A brand name is a competitive advantage all by itself. It taps the emotional needs of customers and creates a bond with them.

- What is the main reason that people trust companies and products? It's a five-letter word beginning with "B."
- Branding gives you an emotional competitive advantage.
- People buy because of emotions no matter how deep their analysis.
- Your most important business asset, even more valuable than your customer mailing list, is your brand.

NINE BRANDS THAT DO IT RIGHT

1. Oprah Winfrey
2. Volkswagen Beetle
3. Star Trek
4. World Wrestling Entertainment
5. Jimmy Buffet
6. Van's Inc.
7. Apple Computer
8. Linux
9. Harley-Davidson

The reasons they do it right:

- People want to be part of a group that's different.
- These brands show daring and determination.
- These brands sell lifestyles.
- These brands have created brand evangelists.
- These brands create customer communities.
- These brands are inclusive.
- These brands promote personal freedom and draw power from their enemies.

Attribute 3: Positioning

Why does your business exist? The answer to that question is your position. The closer that position fills the needs of others, the more primed for success you are. Every single business has a target market. What, specifically, is yours? A target market is made up of unique individuals. Conceptualize just one of them to get insights into what makes them tick. Are there a lot of people like the one you just visualized? If there are, you've got a strong position.

You've also got competition, or you will have it very soon. What is it about your position that will woo their customers onto your customer list? All you've got to be is three things:

1. Unique
2. Desirable
3. Believable

Be those three things and you've got the foundation of a powerful position, a powerful brand. So what is the difference between a position and a brand? Positioning relates to people and how they perceive you. Branding relates to your product or service and how they perceive it. A position is the essence of your product or service; a brand better be the same or you ought to send it packing.

A position creates a brand for you, a path to follow, a willing population of customers. It's much easier to create a brand if you have a clear position. You can't be all things to all people, so what thing or things will you be? And to whom? Those people are wanting to get to know you. They know an appealing brand when they see it. And they know a position that fills their needs. Your ability to position yourself exactly as enough people hope will determine your profits, your brand, and your success.

> Positioning relates to people and how they perceive you. Branding relates to your product or service and how they perceive it.

> It's much easier to create a brand if you have a clear position.

"Positioning is not about finding what the market wants you to be, but about finding out what you are and owning that space."

Attribute 4: Quality

Last century, quality was a marketing strategy. Companies decided that they would provide the utmost in quality and thereby capture a healthy share of market. It worked. Ask Rolls-Royce, Rolex, Ritz-Carlton.

That was last century. This century, if you don't have quality, the nice folks show you to the door. Quality is the price of admission to being in business these days. And if you haven't got it, guerrilla marketing will speed the demise of your company by exposing your shabbiness to more people faster than ever.

In order to have quality, you've got to know what quality is, and most people don't. They think it's something they put into a product or service. Guerrillas know that quality is not something that you put into your product or service, but something that your customers get out of it. Think they give a fig for how many glommets you used in making your gibbet machine? They do not. All they care about is what they get out of your gibbet machine. They are so awed by performance that they're oblivious to where it came from.

That's why most tests of quality have to include the human factor. Yes, the steel must be strong, but it must also be soft and silky and gorgeous and alluring at the same time. Quality is not what it used to be. The more characteristics of quality that you can measure, the more quality you can demonstrate to your customers. So get off of your wavelength and on to theirs to get the true meaning of quality. Seeing it through their eyes is not as important as feeling it in their hearts.

One of the most adorable aspects of quality is its ability to affect price. By offering more perceived value, the visual side of quality, you are able to sell at higher prices—meaning higher profits and more competitors. When there more competitors, the one with the most quality wins the blue ribbon.

> Quality is the price of admission to being in business these days.

> Quality is not something that you put into your product or service, but something that your customers get out of it.

Attribute 5: Location

It used to be that the business with the best location in town was the one at the high traffic location with the outrageously high rent. Now the business with the best location in town is the one at the no-traffic location with no rent because it's just a spare bedroom with a computer that grants you online access.

You no longer need a lavish environment to earn lavish profits. But you do need a hard-working, intimately understood computer. And it helps immensely if you've got a good start on compiling a mailing list you can call your own.

World headquarters is as frequently a kitchen in a rural house as it is a skyscraper in Bombay. It used to be that you needed an expensive office location to be an international company. Now all you need is an e-mail address anywhere where you can connect to the internet.

Do you have to be walking distance from your best customers? Driving distance? Flying distance? Nope. Now all you've got to be is clicking distance. You can do business from your home in LA with another firm in Kuala Lumpur, also operating from a private home. Proximity to customers becomes virtually irrelevant in a world where every location is the best location and anyone who can type has the potential to be an international entrepreneur.

> It used to be that you needed an expensive office location to be an international company. Now all you need is an e-mail address anywhere where you can connect to the internet.

Attribute 6: Opportunities to Upgrade

A customer decides to make a $1,500 purchase from you. He's with you—in person, on the phone, or online—and you let him know that with a second $1,500 purchase, he can get free delivery. He ponders a moment then takes you up on your offer because two $1,500 purchases are probably fragile, not to mention heavy. Bingo! You've upgraded the sale and it didn't cost you a dime. Ever hear of free marketing? You just have. Who better to sell an upgrade or related product or service to than a satisfied, positively thinking, obviously present customer?

The thing to keep in mind is that the people to whom you're selling really and truly want you to suggest a way for them to improve their lives by enlarging their purchase size from you. You'll let them do that and you'll toss in a discount at the same time? How good is

UPGRADES COME IN A WIDE VARIETY OF FORMS

- Delivery
- Installation
- Service contracts
- Extra parts

- Companion pieces
- Deluxe versions
- Complete packages

that? While earning their admiration, you're also earning ours because you deftly put into action this potent way to pump up your profits.

It used to be that when people got upgrades, they felt very special because of the exclusiveness. People still feel special, but they expect an upgrade all along. Do it and do it as much as you can. During a economic downturn, savvy businesses manage to give their profits an upturn by enlarging the size of as many transactions as they can. At the same time, many of them raise their prices substantially. To justify this tactic, they say "during an ugly economy, it doesn't make sense to try and buy the cheapest. Instead, you don't want to make a purchase mistake—and this price helps to assure you of the quality and durability you should be seeking."

Attribute 7: Referral Program

Your greatest source of new customers is old customers. They know you, trust you, have done business with you, and already have a relationship with you. Add to that insight the realization that every customer you have is the center of a network—with an impressive array of people to whom he or she can refer to you: business associates, neighbors, friends, relatives, fellow club-members, even acquaintances.

Be sure you tap this omnipotent referral power of your customers. To get them to refer you, simply ask for referrals. It's that simple and that straightforward. Two or three times a year, you should send brief e-mails to all of your customers, asking the same question, requesting only five names. You'll be very pleased at how many good names you get, and the cost to have such a referral program is the usual investment—time, energy, imagination, and information—but not money.

Train your employees to ask everyone for referrals, explaining that by getting referrals, you're able to keep your costs down. The phone operator at the dentist's office who asks, "Is this appointment for you or for members of your family as well?" understands the simplicity of getting referrals.

If you want to add extra potency to your quest for referrals, ask customers if you can use their names—or best of all, if you can write letters for them to sign in your effort to secure referrals. Always keep in mind that when you seek referrals, you are really doing favors for

CAPTURING REFERRALS

One of the nation's most successful insurance salesmen was interviewed on a radio show. When asked when he begins to get referrals, he answered, "The moment I've made the sale."

He pointed out that the customer is then in a positive mood, wants to share your benefits with others, and is all too willing to help you out. The insurance salesman said, "As soon as the customer signs on my dotted line, I reach into my pocket take take out a small notebook in which I've written the numbers, one, two, three, four, and five. Then I ask him for the names of five people who might benefit from hearing from me. Because I'm only asking for five names—and e-mail addresses when possible—the simplicity of my request combines with the positivity of the moment and I'm usually given five names."

THE MMS PHENOMENON

MMS stands for the Moment of Maximum Satisfaction, which starts the moment the customers makes a purchase and lasts for up until 30 days after that date. This is the period that you will get the most referrals from your customer.

people. You're in business because you believe you're good at what you do. Spreading the word about your prowess is hardly a sin. It's something that guerrillas do as second nature. Be sure you don't brag. Be sure you're totally honest. And be sure you don't hold back on this free way that guerrilla marketers earn their stripes.

Attribute 8: Credibility

> Trust is the leading factor why people patronize a business.

The path to profitability is paved with credibility. Guerrillas do everything in their power to earn this credibility. And there is a lot that they can do. Their web site gives them credibility. So does any advertising that they do. PR stories give it do them, and so do articles they publish, talks they give, interviews they grant.

Because trust is the leading factor why people patronize a business, smart business owners knock themselves out earning this trust because they know it equates with credibility. If you have no credibility, it's going to be very difficult for you to grow, to earn profits, to make sales. People have to believe in you before they'll believe in your products or services.

During the start-up phase of a business, guerrillas make a list of the guerrilla marketing weapons that give them credibility. Then, they set out to employ these weapons in their efforts to make this credibility part of their brand.

In fact, branding is a form of credibility. So is reputation. So are testimonials. As credibility itself is priceless, so are the manners of gaining credibility. You don't have to spend a lot to get a lot of credibility. Everything good that you have done in the past is another component of your credibility. People love to hear of your past actions because it reassures them that you're no fly-by-night operation, that you're for real, and that other people also see you that way.

Contrary to what you may have heard, people do not like to be pioneers. They want to know that others have benefited from doing business with you. Instead of being the first member of the community to do business with you, they want to be the 100th.

> People have to believe in you before they'll believe in your products or services.

INSTANT CREDIBILITY

Can brand-new businesses earn instant credibility? A few days ago, we went into a computer store because we needed some specialized service on our computers. The man we spoke to reassured us that his company could do just what we needed. When we asked how long the company had been in business, we were told, "This is our first day." The service technician must have seen the look of concern on our faces, so he added, "But between the five of us who work here, we have a total of 55 years in business." Credibility takes a long time to build—but there are examples of instant credibility. That's just one of them.

Attribute 9: Testimonials

It's pretty hard to have a galaxy of testimonials the moment you launch your business. So begin to get them the first day you begin operations. When anyone says anything good to you about the way you run your business, ask if they'd consider putting their words into writing. Be honest enough to tell them how much this means to your business because you're brand new.

> When anyone says anything good to you about the way you run your business, ask if they'd consider putting their words into writing.

Testimonials are economical, believable, and versatile. We know one woman who papers a wall of her reception room with testimonials. Some of them are ten years old. That's still another advantage of testimonials—long shelf life.

You can use your testimonials in a variety of ways: as a page on your web site, as part of your sales presentation, as a page in your flipchart, as part of your proposals, or as headlines for your ads and brochures. Here's a hint: The more testimonials you have, the better. Some people, concerned with "white space" in their marketing materials, keep the number of testimonials down to three or four. But profit-minded guerrillas have learned that the more testimonials they include, the more people will be impressed. This is no time for modesty. If ever there was a time to blow your own horn, it's the time you unleash your testimonials to a public that wants to read them, that wants to learn more about you, that cares what others think about you, and that yearn for credibility in the company they're about to patronize.

> *We know of a lady who has used her many testimonial letters to actually wallpaper the entire front reception area of her office.*

Considering their power and ability to motivate others, it's almost too easy to get testimonials. Asking for them is hardly asking for the world. And having them can really mean the world to your business.

SIGNATURE CREDIBILITY

When compiling your list of testimonials, realize that those signed by "T. Smith, Texas" aren't nearly as impressive as those signed by "Julie Townsend, Vice-President, Bank of America."

Attribute 10: Reputation

All you've got to do to attract business simply because of your sterling reputation is handle the hundreds of details of running a business every single day in every kind of situation and do it for at least five years running. It can happen in three years, but before that, your time will be spent laying the foundation for that reputation.

The foundation will include your overcall consistency, your level of service, your ability to handle displeased customers, your way of using the telephone, your neatness, the attitudes of your personnel, and, as if we had to spell this out for you, the quality that customers receive from your offerings. In many companies, value is also part of the equation.

Probably, the most important of these factors in earning a reputation is the first one we mentioned—the consistency you display. One slip-up and you've seriously sabotaged your reputation for such a long time that you'll wince when you learn it. That's the way it goes with reputations. In under a week, a TV spot can evolve from concept to finished commercial earning profits for your business. For a reputation to begin earning those profits takes a whole lot longer, but you must trust us on this one: It's worth the wait.

> The most important of these factors in earning a reputation is the first one we mentioned—the consistency you display.

NEVER LET YOUR GUARD DOWN

We happened to be in Paris the year that front page newspaper coverage was given to the news of a famous restaurant being demoted from four stars to three in the respected *Michelin Guide*. The restaurant critic explained that he ordered a dish in white sauce and thought the sauce was inappropriately seasoned. Zap! One star gone. You can be sure it will take up to a decade to earn it back. The critic elaborated, "When you have the highest possible rating that we bestow, you are not allowed even one chink in the armour."

The method of marketing that money can't buy is your reputation. You don't buy it. You earn it. As powerful as a reputation may be, never forget that it's also fragile. It's far easier to hire a bad representative of your company than a good one. But a bad representative will cost you far more than a good one will earn for you. Remember the delicate nature of your reputation when you hire anyone.

TOP TEN ATTRIBUTES OF A GUERRILLA MARKETER

To quickly review the chapter, here is a complete list of the top ten attributes.

1. Name
2. Branding
3. Positioning
4. Quality
5. Location

6. Opportunities to upgrade
7. Referral program
8. Credibility
9. Testimonials
10. Reputation

7

THE TOP TEN ATTITUDES OF A GUERRILLA MARKETER

You go to a highly respected business school, earn an advanced degree in business, and then find yourself out in the real world where in most cases, your attitude counts more than your education. What do you, an up-and-coming guerrilla, do when reality clashes with booklearning? You find out the attitudes of those guerrillas who are already living your dream, and then you adopt those attitudes for your business. Where do you learn the best attitudes for a guerrilla marketer? You learn them here and you remember that there are more than ten winning attitudes.

Attitude 1: Passion

Passion influences the other attitudes. It fuels your marketing fires, and energizes you beginning in your heart rather than your brain. Passion is

> In the real world, your attitude counts more than your education.

different from enthusiasm because of the heat of the fires. It is different because of the level of the intensity. It's a matter of energy.

Extremely contagious, passion spreads from you to your co-workers, then to your customers, then to their friends. Your passion shows in every aspect of your business. Ideally, your passion is not something that you have to develop. If you're a true guerrilla, it burns within you with the light of its fires guiding you in the right direction and solving your problems.

> *"There are two great days in a person's life—the day we were born and the day we discover why."*
>
> —WILLIAM BARCLAY

> Passion influences the other attitudes. It fuels your marketing fires, and energizes you beginning in your heart rather than your brain.

You already know about passion because it has motivated you to take marketing seriously and to be bright enough to start at the beginning rather than the middle, where most businesses start. One of your toughest jobs will be to find people who bring the same passion to the table. You might not be able to do that. But it doesn't bother you because you know you have enough passion for the entire company.

But do you? Will that passion generate energy even in a tough economy, even after business downturns, even after loss of a key customer or supplier? Will it be there eight years from now? If you've got the right stuff in the passion department, all the answers are yes. And eight years from now—oh boy!—you just light up at the ways you'll be able to exercise your passion then!

> *Take the passion test: go to www.thepassiontest.com.*

Attitude 2: Generosity

We investigated this attitude in detail as Trait 7 back in Chapter 2. We're not going to repeat ourselves, but we'd be remiss if we didn't

THE FINE LINE OF GENEROSITY

We spent the past few weeks furniture shopping, or more accurately, furniture buying. Visiting store after store, we were treated to a broad array of good and bad attitudes. We realized that if the showroom is too generous—"We'll give you those two decorator pillows, that rug, and the ottoman if you buy today . . . and we'll toss in free delivery,"—that made us wonder if everything we were buying was overpriced to begin with. Then there was the opposite. "The floor model of this recliner sofa is the only model that's on sale right now. To get the fabric you want on that sofa would cost three times as much as this sale price." Although that was probably the truth, it didn't demonstrate the store's devotion to generosity, so we walked.

include it in this list of tep ten business attitudes. It's included because it's so rare.

You've got to talk that fine line between too generous and not generous enough if you embrace the attitude generosity. Embracing an attitude of overall generosity means that you not only practice generosity, but that it delights you to do so.

> Embracing an attitude of overall generosity means that you not only practice generosity, but that it delights you to do so.

Attitude 3: Speed

Time is NOT money. You read it here first, unless you read it already in every other guerrilla marketing book since the 1990s. Instead, time is life, and your customers know it. If they sense that you're wasting their time and don't respect it enough, they'll find a competitor of yours that wouldn't dream of wasting their time.

Speed doesn't necessarily mean racing all over your office or store. But it does mean moving fast whenever there's the option of moving slowly. Let your customers see, hear, and sense how oriented you are to speed. That will attract them as well as give them some cogent words to say if they're engaging in word-of-mouth marketing.

> *"The electronics store we shop at has all its speakers in one demonstration room so we could sit on an easy chair and listen to many rather than walk and listen to just a few, saving both our time and our feet."*

Time is NOT money; time is life.

Recall that the cost of speed is zero. It's just a matter of attitude, and not just attitude on your part. When you hire and train people, be sure they understand the precious nature of time as well as you do and are just as willing to work fast in an effort to save the precious time of your precious customers. Your business will operate at the speed of your slowest employee. Bottlenecks are toxic to companies dedicated to speed. If your customers have to wait in line anywhere—at your store, at a cash register, on the phone, or online—don't be surprised if they become ex-customers.

Speed is not yet taken for granted, but pretty darned soon it will be. Until that day, your attitude of speed and never wanting a customer to wait gives you a competitive advantage. Keep your eyes open for businesses that adopt a time-based strategy. You'll be seeing more and more of them as more and more customers come to realize that time is life.

Attitude 4: Sincere Caring

We'll bet you know the difference between caring and sincere caring. Customers expect caring. They do not expect sincere caring. Customers aren't necessarily made to feel good by caring. They feel very good when they experience sincere caring. Caring doesn't show. Sincere caring is very obvious.

If you adopt an attitude of sincere caring, it will shorten the time before you have a multitude of warm relationships. As with the other attitudes in this top ten, sincere caring helps your company the most if everyone who has customer contact displays it. If just you display it, that's nice, but that's not overwhelmingly nice.

Businesses that demonstrate caring are the kind that might or might not be there for you in a pinch or when you have trouble with your purchase. Businesses that demonstrate sincere caring will always be there for you in times of strife and will happily go to bat for you with top management or a recalcitrant supplier. They actually go out of their way to prove that they care. You can tell them by the way they ask questions and look you right in the eyes, by the way they attentively listen to your answers and have an intelligent response to them.

> *How does an attitude of sincere caring come about?*
> *In two ways:*
> *1. Brilliant hiring*
> *2. Brilliant training*

If you accomplish the first, it will be that much easier to accomplish the second because you have role models and potential trainers. One of the most winning aspects of all of these attitudes is the cost. There is none.

Still another winning aspect is the profit potential of these attitudes. There is plenty. Mark our words.

Attitude 5: Honest Friendliness

I'm guessing that you know what we mean by "honest friendliness." There's a world of difference between it and phony friendliness. Almost everyone has a radar that indicates whether the person talking to them really means what he says or is just going through the motions.

Listen, it's tough to deal with prospects and customers hour after hour, day after day. Most salespeople wear down in the process, but they can't leave the office. They want to keep their jobs, so they loosen into a state of false friendliness. Notice their lack of eye contact, absence of enthusiasm, lackadaisical body language, and half-hearted smile. They definitely know the words, but you just can't hear the music.

When you have a staff of trained guerrillas who are able to practice honest friendliness whenever they're on the job, your prospects and customers can hear the music. They can have a meaningful dialogue with your salespeople. They trust them. They buy from them. How much did this cost? You know it cost nothing but exceptional care on your part during the hiring process and nonstop conscientiousness when it came to training.

In a perfect world, whatever that is, your people wouldn't have to be trained and you wouldn't have to be so cautious when hiring. But as we said earlier, many salespeople get tired and suffer from energy meltdown at times during the day. To combat that reality, hiring and training will be keys to your success. Yes, there are honestly friendly people out there, people who are just plain fascinated with other people. Cherish these people. Hire them and reward them well. But don't expect them to be easy to find. You should be on the constant lookout for bright and shiny people. But we think that what the others don't have at birth, they can get from you.

It's obvious that there's a world of similarities between sincere caring and honest friendliness. Both are rare. And that's precisely why companies that are blessed to have them on staff are rare themselves and provide an atmosphere that makes customers feel comfortable in your surroundings and confident in your business.

More and more, it's becoming recognized that one of the secrets to success in business is to create a pleasant buying environment. That doesn't necessarily mean a dazzling showroom. It means people who make prospects and customers feel good throughout the entire experience.

One of the secrets to success in business is to create a pleasant buying environment.

MAKING CONTACT

Years ago, the Bahamian Islands were experiencing a slump in tourism. It seemed that the locals resented the tourists, the tourists sensed it, and started choosing other places to take their vacations.

To combat this, the Bahamian government started teaching their young children in school how important tourism was to the country's economy, and that tourism is what enabled their parents to be able to afford to buy them things. They taught the children to make an effort to be friendly to the tourists, helping them feel welcome, by greeting everyone they met, making direct eye contact, and giving them a big smile.

After some time, tourism made a comeback in the Bahamas, and if you travel there, you will notice the friendliness, especially among the children and now young adults.

The Bahamian government had learned the business value of sincere friendliness.

Who are those people? You knew the answer before we even wrote it here: people who exhibit sincere caring and honest friendliness.

Attitude 6: Neatness

Two of the most successful business operations in the history of earth are Disney and McDonald's. Everyone who has visited any Disney property is impressed by the cleanliness, the neatness, the absence of any mess. One of Disney's policies is to be sure the restrooms are cleaned every 15 minutes.

What are the things that people like most about McDonald's? Number one is clean restrooms. Number two is good French fries. You'd think that their success had something to do with hamburgers and prices. But you'd only be half right. Clean restrooms are number one on the list. And the fries are pretty darned good.

KEEP IT CLEAN

Once, we spent a chunk of time at Epcot in Disney World in Orlando. We decided to sit down and spend some of that time observing people littering. Sure enough, the visitors littered with the best of them, but the litter didn't remain on the ground more than five minutes. It seemed that Disney employees appeared from behind shrubbery or dropped from clouds to make the litter disappear. Disney knows that neatness is an all-day endeavor.

What's the main reason that women select the service stations they do? Answer: clean restrooms. Nothing about octane or prices. Everything about neatness.

> When people see that your premises are neat, they assume that you run the rest of your business that way. When people see the premises are sloppy, they figure that's how they'll be treated in a pinch.

When people see that your premises are neat, they assume that you run the rest of your business that way. When people see the premises are sloppy, they figure that's how they'll be treated in a pinch. You'd be appalled if you knew how many people never make a purchase in a place that hints of dirt—anywhere.

Interesting fact: One of the world's biggest neat freaks was Ray Kroc, founder of McDonald's. Another world-class neat freak was Walt Disney. It's notable to realize that their inherent neatness was one of the reasons for their outstanding success.

You won't hear the word "neatness" in most marketing lectures, even at the best universities. But you will in the marketing plans of McDonald's, Disney, Nordstrom, and a host of others. It is our hope that you become one of those others, because neatness is an attitude that equates very closely with profitability.

Attitude 7: Telephone Demeanor

Of all the minority groups on earth, the most special to you are the people who call your business on the telephone. Are your customers

KEEP A SMILE IN YOUR VOICE

Once, we were called into Midas Muffler Shops because management was dismayed at its inability to make appointments with callers. Midas was getting 100 percent of its initial contacts by the phone, which is wonderful, but it was converting only 71 percent of those callers into appointments, which is terrible. It meant staff was dropping the ball 29 percent of the time.

While surveying the shops in person, we couldn't help but notice that most of the time the ringing telephone was answered by a person who obviously didn't want to be on the phone. That person was too busy, in a conversation with a customer, in a bad mood, or an introvert. Whatever the reason, the person answering the phone didn't want to be doing that—and it showed. No wonder so many callers failed to make an appointment for a new muffler.

We suggested a telephone training program. It would take only half a day. Midas was so warm to the idea that it instituted a new rule: "You can't answer the phone at a Midas Muffler Shop unless you've taken this telephone training." Within six months, Midas began converting 94 percent of all callers into finished appointments. That represents over $10 million in profits, yet the cost was negligible.

We pointed out to the Midas people the importance of outstanding customer service and explained that customer service begins with the phone. We emphasized the need for warmth and friendliness, for patience and the ability to never seem to be in a hurry. We told them that bad moods are illegal on the phone and that introverts are not encouraged to answer the phone. Simple guidelines. Easy-to-listen-to advice. Common sense. It was presented so clearly that only one training session was needed. This was not information that had to be pounded into someone's head. It was straightforward advice that was easy to remember and easy to implement.

made to feel like interruptions of your business or like the reason you're in business the first place? All too often, potential customers call a business, are treated discourteously by a busy operator, then cross it off their list as a source of what they want to buy.

Anyone who answers your phone just has to be trained in the proper way to treat callers. Those callers should hear a smile in the voice of the operator, sense a desire to please, and made to feel important.

We can't emphasize strongly enough that you can institute, then implement the same kind of telephone training. You can transform all your callers into friends, and many of them into customers. Do it right at the start of running your business. It's the guerrilla way.

The same warm attitude should be apparent on your electronic telephone answering equipment: friendly message, caring attitude, and helpful information.

Attitude 8: Value

Is value really an attitude? Or is it only an attribute that propels business? Of course, it's both. Just because you happen to offer a sleek new automobile rated highest by the most respected automotive reviewers yet priced at $3,000 lower than your closest competition, does that mean your value along with your quality, service, and selection are enough to take your propects over the top and onto your customer list? Barely. So give yourself a boost by exuding quality in your décor, attire, interior furniture, and restrooms. There you are, selling $75,000 cars, and here are we reminding you to clean the toilets.

It is that exquisite attention to detail that can make you confident enough to radiate confidence in your marketing. That's a value attitude—it showcases the real value that's up ahead. To communicate it, act like a winner. Assume that everyone shares your attitude and knows how good you are. That assumption will make value part of your perception.

If value does, indeed, become part of your very essence, good things will begin to happen. You'll discover that it's easier to sell on value than on price. You'll see that the price shoppers aren't as loose or mellow as the value shoppers. Which group do you suppose would best qualify for an enlarged price transaction?

People who purchase for considerations of value are seeking reputation, brand awareness, and safety, all the usual niceties, plus a fair price. Fair is a low price plus the person's perception of your value. Their perception will rise in accordance with how lavish you are with your details, related to your product or service, or related to you or your company. You'd be amazed if you knew the things that are perceived as value. Not surprisingly, high price is among the leaders.

> It's easier to sell on value than on price; the price shoppers aren't as loose or mellow as the value shoppers.

VALUED PERCEPTION

We were involved with a national hair conditioner product with sagging sales. It was packaged in a very handsome and beautifully shaped bottle, but the contents were pretty much the same as all the other conditioners in the category. We tripled the price. Sales more than tripled. People figured that if it's so expensive, it must be good. We do not advise that strategy except to clue you in that raising prices is not the worst thing in the world.

No product category in America is led by the lowest-priced brand. We just want you to realize that if you sell solely on price, other price-cutters will constantly woo your price-conscious customers away. If you sell on value, you have a much better chance of maintaining a profitable long-term relationship.

Attitude 9: Easy to Do Business With

You've often heard it said—at least we have—that it's easier to deal with failure than success. We've seen that be true many times. Over-expansion, naïve hiring, poor financial management, overpromising, silly time management, and unreasonable egos—those are a sampling of the perils of success.

The perils of failure are more fixable.

ABLE TO SAY YES

A remarkably successful young company had doubled its sales each year since it started in 1972. At a board of directors meeting in 1991, the chairman announced that 1992 would be devoted to no growth. The gasp from the directors was clearly audible. He explained that the company was no longer able to say yes to every customer request, no longer able to provide next-day service, and in short, had become difficult to do business with. "We'll be devoted in 1992 to saying yes to all requests, providing next-day service 365 days a year," announced the president. "We'll become easy to do business with once again."

Perhaps it's because the company became so customer compliant that the following year they were purchased by a *Fortune* 500 company for a staggering sum of money.

If you can winnow out a lesson in this tale about the value of superlative customer service, your company will gain from it. If you haven't, we feel compelled, since this is the dawn of your guerrilla marketing ventures with your business, to remind you of something that becomes more of what you should be about each time you're exposed to the thought.

First, think this thought: YOU. Your business is not about that person. That person helps make things smooth and pleasant for the truly important people, your prospects and your customers. Those are the one who count. They're the ones you must empathize with at every opportunity. There is no way on earth that you can't arrange to say yes to their requests. They want next-day service? You find a way for them to get it—and for the other people like them to get it.

It's easier to deal with failure than success.

We tremble when we call a bank. We know we will be treated courteously by a machine then put on hold, and sometimes perma-hold. There's a good chance we'll be transferred at least once and an off chance we'll be dropped from the line and forced to begin the process again. Many banks are not very easy to do business with.

Your mission is to be very easy to do business with. People might not do a dance of joy when they're about to call you, but they don't tremble either. And more calls equal more profits.

Attitude 10: Flexibility

What might be an effort for you is now a given, an act of kindness taken for granted by your customers. They know their parents didn't have it like this, but hey, it's a competitive world, and you've got to offer flexibility or perish. Inflexible things become brittle and break, while flexible things have long life spans and attract customers who will patronize your business for a long time—or at least as long as you consistently demonstrate your flexibility.

> Offer flexibility or perish; inflexible things become brittle and break.

JUST BE FLEXIBLE

Phil Knight, chief of everything at Nike, provides a perfect example of this flexibility. A woman was seated on a plane next to him. She mentioned that she had MS and always had trouble finding properly designed shoes. Phil Knight, living by his "Just do it" mantra, took a meticioulour meas-urement of the woman's foot and lower leg, along with her mailing address. Three months later, a package arrived at the woman's door. It was a pair of one-of-a-kind Nike shoes designed for one individual with MS. Phil Knight demonstrated gold medal flexibility—and at no charge.

It's crucial to know about flexibility at the outset of your guerrilla marketing attack. By starting with it, you won't be knocked off your chair the first time you're asked to prove yours. Although you won't be asked to put your flexibility on display many times a year, you must have it ready to rumble at all times.

Flexibility has more to do with service and product than it does with price. It has more to do with timing than it does with money. You can probably survive whether or not you have price flexibility, but you'll gain priceless word of mouth if you have service or product flexibility. Whenever we've experienced it, we told literally hundreds of people—simply to show them that small companies aren't the only ones that strut their flexibility stuff.

TOP TEN ATTITUDES OF A GUERRILLA MARKETER

To quickly review the chapter, here is a complete list of the top ten attitudes.

1. Passion	6. Neatness
2. Generosity	7. Telephone demeanor
3. Speed	8. Value
4. Sincere caring	9. Easy to do business with
5. Honest friendliness	10. Flexibility

8

GUERRILLA
MARKETING DEFINED

Marketing is everything you do to promote your business, from the moment you conceive of it, to the point at which customers buy your product or service and begin to patronize your business on a regular basis. The key words to remember are "everything" and "regular basis." Marketing is all contact that you or anyone within your organization has with anyone outside of your organization. It includes:

- The name of your business
- Determining whether you will be selling a product or service
- Method of manufacture or servicing
- Colors, size, and shape or your product
- Packaging
- Location of your business

- Advertising
- Public relations
- Sales training
- Sales presentation
- Telephone inquiries
- Problem solving
- Growth plan
- Referral plan
- Follow-up

Marketing is a complex process that requires your full attention. *Marketing is a circle* that starts with your idea for generating revenue and completes itself when you have the patronage of repeat and referral business.

> Guerrilla marketing means going after conventional goals using unconventional means.

What Is Guerrilla Marketing?

Guerrilla marketing means going after conventional goals using unconventional means. It means that in marketing, your main investments should be time, energy, imagination, and information—not

---

SMART THINKING

There was once little store in the middle of two giant stores. One day the little store owner was dismayed to come into work and find that each of the two larger stores had hung huge banners outside announcing "Grand Opening Sale—prices slashed 50 percent" and "Monster Clearance Sale—prices slashed 75 percent." Worse yet, each banner was larger than his own store.

The little store owner, being a guerrilla, and knowing he couldn't compete with those kind of prices, responded by creating and displaying his own banner, which simply read . . . "Main Entrance."

---

money. If you want to invest money, that's cool, but you don't really have to if you don't want to.

The story in the Smart Thinking sidebar is a good example of how guerrilla marketing can work.

Your Main Marketing Investment

Guerrilla marketing advises that your primary investment in marketing should not be money, but rather time, energy, imagination, and information. Guerrilla marketing also clarifies and simplifies marketing in a way no other marketing discipline ever has.

Although guerrilla marketing is geared to small business, with its roots in one-person and homebased businesses, more and more large corporations are embracing the wisdom of guerrilla marketing. After all, the small guys aren't the only ones who ought to benefit from it, the big guys also need all the help they can get.

The truth is that guerrilla marketing helps all businesses reduce their marketing expenses to get the maximum payoff from their marketing investments. It removes the unnecessary games from marketing and focuses on the thing that really fills the vaults.

> Guerrilla marketing advises that your primary investment in marketing should not be money, but rather time, energy, imagination, and information.

How Guerrillas Measure

Guerrilla marketing stresses different yardsticks than old-fashioned measures of performance. It pays little heed to sales, store traffic, web site hits, and turnover, concentrating instead on profits, profits, and profits. We have known more than a few business owners who set sales records, while at the same time losing their shirts. It is not about sales records. It is about profits. If you could switch on a neon sign in your brain, it should say "profits," for the other yardsticks lead you astray.

That's not your fate. You know what to watch when the ball comes speeding in. You've got to develop this skill at the very outset of your business. It's part of the foundation of starting to launch a

> Guerrilla marketing pays little heed to sales, store traffic, web site hits, and turnover, concentrating instead on profits.

TAKE CAUTION WITH SALES

A mattress dealer had a brainstorm. People love things that are free, so he had a "Free-for-All" sale. With every purchase of a king- or queen-size bed, the purchaser got two free pillows, a mattress pad, a blanket, a comforter, and a top sheet, bottom sheet, and pillowcases. The sale brought in large numbers of people from the moment the store opened on a Saturday morning until it closed Sunday at midnight. The revenue was startling and the store was nearly empty. When the boss told his inventory supply manager that he wanted to order the same number of beds in inventory, he was told that they could probably sell that many beds plus another ten now that they had their sleep presentation so buttoned up. Next, the boss told his money manager that they'd be repeating the Free-for-All sale for the next three weekends.

That money manager looked glum at the good news. "We lose $109 every time we make a sale. We lost our shirts last week with all the things we gave away. We broke two records—highest sales ever and biggest loss ever suffered."

guerrilla marketing attack and defend yourself from attacks by ever-more-brilliant competitors. Game on.

But it's not a game. It's for money. Your money. Real money. You need skills you've never needed before. One elusive trait leading the parade of skills you'll need is the ability to know profits or lack of profits when you see them.

Don't Change Behavior, Benefit By It

To do this, you've got to know what people need and want, and how to benefit by their behavior. So guerrilla marketing cozies up closer and closer to psychology, which gains credibility faster than it loses it.

How much does it help you to know what to talk about to prospects? The answer is *how they'll feel after they've made the purchase.*

If you talk about this to them, you'll be saying what they want and need to hear. Approach your prospects on the logical level by talking specifics and whisper to them on the emotional level by talking about their feelings.

Focus on Excellence

Guerrilla marketing allows you to get close to your prospects from any of 360 degrees. The more you truly are fascinated with people, the more likely you'll succeed with it. This strategy book on marketing urges you to focus on a specialty and resist the desire to diversify. Focus on providing more excellence, not more stuff.

> Approach your prospects on the logical level by talking specifics and whisper to them on the emotional level by talking about their feelings.

NAME GAME

A well-known soda company decided that its name meant "beverages" so it opened a winery. After it lost several million dollars it determined that its name didn't mean beverages after all; maybe it only meant "soft drinks."

Likewise, a well-known baby food company decided that its name meant "babies," so it started a line of baby clothes and baby furniture. In turn, it also lost several million dollars until it, too, came to the conclusion that its name really only meant "baby food."

Growing, Guerrilla Style

As devoted as you are to your craft, apply yourself to achieving inexpensive and intelligent growth. Strive to enlarge the size of each transaction with things like:

- Service contracts
- Extra technology
- Deluxe versions
- Companion items on sale

- Monthly cleaning
- Whatever your customers might need at the time of sale

The cost to capitalize on this pregnant moment is nothing. The rewards are generous—especially if you're as imaginative as we think you are.

In a continuing effort to practice inexpensive and intelligent marketing, you stay in touch with your past customers—thanking them for their business, asking if they need any help from you or if you can answer any questions from them, offering them companion products and services that tie in with their original purchase, even offering them exceptional values on product and services available from your fusion marketing partners.

Monthly or quarterly, they hear from you—receive a special offer from you, receive a free gift from you—very aware that you're staying in touch and maintaining top-of-the-mind awareness. When your customers need or want something, they'll put in a call to you. Stay in touch forever, and you'll mutually benefit forever.

Those same customers are the centers of networks. Each one is the center of a network of family, friends, business associates, neighbors, club members, and golf or fishing buddies. That means that each one is a powerful link to more people a lot like them, and those people are linked to a lot of people, too. Starting out a guerrilla marketing attack means getting referral names right at the outset and building the list of those names on a regular basis.

Three Different Directions at Once

Grow your business geometrically, not just linearly. By striving to grow your business in three different directions at the same time—more profitable transactions, more regular transactions, and referral transactions—plus adding new customers the expensive old-fashioned way, you'll be developing the sensible and powerful habits of a marketing guerrilla.

The Follow-Up Follies

Guerrilla marketing erects monuments to follow-up, honors it, and practices it. We suffer from economic pain with the knowledge that of all that hard-earned business—business that took a lot of time, energy, imagination, and information to build—a stunning 68 percent of it is ultimately lost due to customers being ignored after the sale. It's so easy to stay in touch with them. But staying in touch just doesn't happen. And countless profits dance away before being born.

Enter guerrilla marketing with its laser-focused dedication to keeping customers after the sale, proving it by staying in close touch with those customers, and then selling them something that intensifies the relationship. That alone can pay a lot of bills. It won't cost much money because as a start-up superstar, you've been collecting names and e-mail addresses—and that's where the gold is hidden.

It's pretty simple to follow up on sales with automated e-mail, e-mail itself, postcards, phone calls, surface mail, and overnight carriers. It's never been easier for both the sender and the receiver, but still, 68 percent of business lost in America is lost due to a ho-hum attitude by the seller after the sale. Your profit can soar if only you use an inexpensive autoresponder to automatically and effectively breathe vitality into your follow-up program.

Nonguerrillas think that marketing is over once the sale had taken place. Guerrillas know that that is the moment that the real profits are determined. One business owner might click the money into his account and forget you forever. Another might have arranged it so that his auto-responder sent you a thank-you note within two minutes of receiving your order, plus a coupon good for a generous discount next week. This gets followed, always automatically, by enticing purchase ideas that add a substantial amount of profits to his back account.

> A stunning 68 percent of business is ultimately lost due to customers being ignored after the sale.

Natural Bonding

If you think that our penchant for follow-up keeps us away from the herd, wait till you read how our natural bonding patterns relegate us to still another maverick group. In business, as in war, competitors strive to eliminate each other. That's probably a good thing in war, but not such a good thing in business. Guerrillas are inclined to think more about cooperation than competition.

They walk down the street and see businesses on both sides. While the guerrilla in war has ample opportunities to zap the competition, the guerrilla in business has ample opportunities to learn of those businesses. If any of them have prospects such as he has and has standards that would not sully his reputation, he suggests an arrangement to trade prospect names and e-mails each month. Possibly one of the two know an accountant or small business insurance expert. Invite those people in. Clubs where leads are traded, not sold, are populated by guerrillas, who find them abundant sources of profits as well as abundant chances to help his allies. Notice that now, they are allies. A few pages back, they were competitors.

You'll make more money in fusion marketing arrangements with compatible people than you would by obliterating them as competitors. New competitors sprout like thorny weeds. New allies are precious and long term.

> *You see fusion marketing at work in the commercials that seem to be for McDonald's, then switch to being spots for Coca-Cola, and end up being plugs for the latest Disney movie.*

However, you see fusion marketing much more commonly with small businesses, such as the video store that hands out discount coupons for the local cleaner who hands out discount coupons for the video store. It's so obvious, it makes our teeth itch!

Guerrillas actively seek fusion marketing partners not for long-term relationships, but for single projects that are never repeated if

| Guerrillas are inclined to think more about cooperation than competition. |

| Guerrillas actively seek fusion marketing partners. |

A LESSON FROM GEESE

Have you ever wondered why migrating geese fly in formation? As each bird flaps its wings, it creates uplift for the bird following. In a V formation, the whole flock adds at least 71 percent more flying range than if each bird flew alone. Whenever a goose falls out of formation, it suddenly feels the drag and resistence of trying to fly alone and it quickly gets back into formation.

Like geese, businesses that share a common direction and sense of community can get where they are going quicker and easier than those who try to go it alone. We are no longer living in the age of the lone wolf entrepreneur, independent and proud of it.

When a lead goose gets tired, it rotates back into the formation and another goose flies at the point position. If business owners had as much sense as geese, they would realize that success depends on fusion marketing partners, working as teams, taking turns doing the hard tasks, exchanging leads, and sharing their marketing budgets.

nobody profits but are repeated often if three groups profit: you, your ally, and your customers.

Me versus You

Click over to anyone's web page and you'll see sections entitled "About Us," "About Our History," "Our Mission," "Our Management," and a lot more. Those sections are talking about the wrong topic. They're talking about the owner of the web site: me. When people visit your web site, they don't want to visit a person who talks about himself—me, me, me,—they want to visit a person who will talk about them—you, you, you. Nothing personal, but people don't care a fig about your company. They always care a ton about themselves.

Guerrilla web sites and guerrilla marketing materials don't start with words about themselves, but rather words about their visitors.

> When people visit your web site, they don't want to visit a person who talks about himself–me, me, me,–they want to visit a person who will talk about them–you, you, you.

It's the "me" versus "you" that separates a traditional web site from a guerrilla web site.

Every sentence should be about the visitor, every sentence with a "you." No sentences should be about "me," no sentences with a "me" or a "we." It's the "me" versus "you" that separates a traditional web site from a guerrilla web site. Here's a valuable hint: If you start out talking "you" words and avoid "me" words, you'll be starting out in the right direction. If you start out talking about anything else, you'll be talking yourself out of a sale and a relationship.

Look carefully at the copy on the main page of your web site or at a version you plan to put up in that esteemed position. Every single sentence can be addressed to the visitor to your site. Try it. Try seeing everything from a visitor's point of view. Studies prove that internet visitors have one paramount goal: to accomplish something. Do everything in your power to help them accomplish that goal.

See the entire process, from clicking to your site to clicking away from it (face up to it, eventually, visitors have to click away from you, even if they bought like money was going out of style) from a visitor's point of view. Talk to her about it. Tell her what to do first, what to do next, and what to do after that. Assume nothing. Most visitors appreciate all the help they get. Anticipate what they're thinking but guide them into doing something. If you talk about them throughout the process, it will be much easier for them to make a wise and informed purchase decision.

Guerrilla marketing goes against one of the basic tenets of old-style marketing, the one that advised business owners to take from customers and prospects all that they could, and give them nothing beyond what they purchased.

Think in terms of giving, not taking. The prime purposes of marketing is to educate your prospects and customers on how to achieve their goals.

The deal with guerrilla marketing is to think in terms of giving, not taking. Remember that one of the prime purposes of marketing is to educate your prospects and customers on how to achieve their goals. That clear purpose can be accomplished very simply by availing yourself of the free treasures offered by Google and public domain materials. Provide valuable information to your list. Do it by e-mail and by putting it up on your web site. First comes the web site with the treasure, then comes the e-mail to your list. Offer the people on that list a special report, an e-book, or a newsletter, and charge them nothing. Educate them to succeed at whatever their goal may be, one goal per campaign. By thinking of what you can give, you'll end up on the positive side of the ledger in many respects.

Coming Up with a Combination

Your job, as a start-up guerrilla, is to be aware of all 200 weapons not just the ten we discussed in Chapter 7, experiment with many of them, discard the losers, and end up with a short list of marketing combinations that have proven themselves in action for your business. See Chapter 12 for the list of all 200.

The days of single-weapon marketing have faded into history. Today, and tomorrow, marketing combinations are going to rule the roost. There will be new weapons all the time—such as blogs and publish-on-demand books—so there will be new marketing combinations all the time. You're going to have to make yours more lethal on a regular basis. By lethal, we mean profitable, and that job of making yours more lethal is one of the most important jobs you have. It's

> The days of single-weapon marketing have faded into history. Today, and tomorrow, marketing combinations are going to rule the roost.

FIVE PRICELESS GEMS

1. Advertising doesn't work.

2. Having a web site doesn't work.

3. Doing PR doesn't work.

4. If you advertise, have a web site, and a PR strategy, all three will work because they'll help each other work.

5. The only thing that works these days are marketing combinations.

a continuous process that will generate new profits in new ways for the life of your business. You may end up with a winning combination in a short time, a matter of weeks. But more likely, it will take you several months to hit paydirt.

Just don't stop there.

Relationships Over Sales

At the end of the month, the nonguerrilla company will count up money. The guerrilla organization will count up relationships. "How many new relationships did we establish this month?" That organization knows that *relationships are the key to long-term profits.*

They know it's much easier to win a customer than to forge a relationship. Because they're guerrillas, they do both. Many ill-fated companies do just half the job. You should constantly be thinking, "What can I do to intensify my relationships with my customers?" You'll surprise yourself with the variety of answers: Send them a newsletter, give them a gift, take them to lunch, take them to the ballgame (or the opera). Never fail to distinguish between your B list customers, who should be treated like royalty, and your A list customers, who should be treated like family.

As a courtship takes time to ripen before the relationship flourishes, so it is in commerce, where again, human beings are at both ends of the equation. Keep in mind that people want relationships. They don't resent your efforts to get closer to them and to curry their favor. Actually, they like the whole idea of relationships and are happy when you prove that you want one. So give them what they want, a long-term, mutually rewarding relationship. The best place to start one is during the start of your guerrilla marketing program.

Cuddle Up with Technology

The big revolution in technology is not that it's become more powerful or more versatile, but that it's become easier to use, more small-biz

> At the end of the month, the nonguerrilla company will count up money. The guerrilla organization will count up relationships.

friendly than ever. These guerrillas know that the real 700-pound guerrilla is a bug—a bug about technology. The guerrilla knows how to use it to empower his business, to render better customer service, and to earn higher profits. Best of all, it's easier than ever to use.

If you suffer from technophobia, run, don't walk, to the nearest technoshrink because technophobia is fatal these days. Guerrillas are technocozy because they aren't daunted by the thought of pushing a button or clicking a mouse. Instead of being intimidated and befuddled by the internet, they eventually become attracted to its simplicity and learn to use it for what it really is: magic.

> If you suffer from technophobia, run, don't walk, to the nearest technoshrink because technophobia is fatal these days.

The Power of One

Although you may be aiming your messages at millions, those messages are read one person at a time. There may have been teams of talent creating your marketing, but that marketing will be processed one person at a time.

Copywriting wisdom reminds you that when writing copy, direct it at one individual, no matter how many will be seeing or hearing it.

NANOCASTING

"Nanocasting" is a new word coined by Errol Smith, a brilliant guerrilla marketing associate of ours. To understand nanocasting, imagine you have a product, say Viagra for example. If you were to advertise your product on national televison, that would be called "broadcasting." If you were to advertise it on a cable channel that is geared toward men, let's say Spike or ESPN, that would be considered "narrowcasting." If you refined your marketing to be shown on television during shows that are geared toward men's health, that would be referred to as "microcasting." But the most precision type of marketing would be to target your advertisements to men's televison, on health channels, on episodes that are dealing specifically with the problem of erectile dysfunction. Now that's NANOCASTING!

| Market to individuals rather than groups. |

Guerrilla marketing wisdom reminds you to strive to market to individuals rather than groups. Big business tends to market to big groups—the bigger the group, the better. Small business is well counseled to market to individuals or, if to a group, the smaller the group the better.

The idea is to think cellular. A big population of small cells exists in your community, industry, and interest group. Target the center of each cell, knowing your message will radiate to others. Once again, respect the power of the individual.

The Intentional Guerrilla

In big companies, marketing includes only the big guns: television, online, radio, newspapers, magazines, direct mail, telemarketing, and a handful more. But of the many points of contact that you have with a prospect, there are a whole lot more ways you interact with a customer.

Detail is the middle name of many a marketing guerrilla. Details are what customers notice, especially the absence of details. Points of contact rarely found in big biz marketing strategies are how your telephone is answered, the outgoing message on your phone, what callers hear when you put them on hold, your Yellow Pages ad, and your business cards. A few of them are expensive. Most of them are ignored by many businesses.

| Details are what customers notice, especially the absence of details. |

The neatness of your premises, friendliness of your employees, and your overall vibe communicate a whole lot of good things or bad things about you. You'd think that the condition of your restroom is no part of marketing. But just the opposite is true, as we explained earlier. Be messy in there and your customers will think you're messy everywhere.

Because big businesses often overlook details, guerrillas have an edge. By identifying every place where there is any customer contact, guerrillas can add details that would add pleasure to the purchase experience. Businesses that fail to do this run unintentional operations.

What is planned is executed. What is not planned is often lost in the shuffle.

Guerrilla businesses are run intentionally. No details are ignored. All points of contact with customers are smooth. Because these contacts are free, it requires no financial investment to sail an intentional ship. These details of marketing don't get covered in marketing textbooks, classes, or seminars, but they are marketing whether you like it or not.

> By identifying every place where there is any customer contact, guerrillas can add details that would add pleasure to the purchase experience.

All You Want Is a Little Yes

It's tougher than ever to make a sale with marketing. You can draw attention and build awareness. But making the sale is just too complex, slow, and frustrating. That's why so many guerrillas have discovered the real joy of gaining consent. Some experts estimate that at any given moment, 4 percent of the U.S. population wants your product now. Another 4 percent want it soon. But the other 92 percent—they'd prefer that you'd leave them alone; they're otherwise occupied.

In his brilliant book, *Permission Marketing* (Simon & Schuster, 1999), Seth Godin advises us to go for consent instead of the sale, then broaden that consent. He relates the following story:

> Go for consent instead of the sale, then broaden that consent.

A woman owned a summer camp in upstate New York. Like other summer camps owners, she ran teeny little ads in the camping directories found in the rear of many Eastern magazines. Did they attempt to sell the camping experience? They did not. All they attempted to do was get people to send for her free DVD. She also had a booth at one of the camping shows that spring up in the Northeast like spring flowers. Does she try to selling the camping experience with her booth? Nope. She only tries to get interested parties to leave with one of her free DVDs.

The people view the DVDs. They see happy campers, trained counselors, beautiful scenery, and lovely equipment. Does that DVD attempt to sell the camping experience? You know it didn't. All it did was try to get viewers to call the camp owners' toll-free number and request an in-home consultation. Some 82 percent of people requested one. Of those, the majority signed up their child for that summer, and not just that summer, but the summer after that and the summer after that. The parents also signed up the brothers and sisters of the camper-to-be. And you've got to figure that a lot of cousins and classmates also signed up. So even though the woman did not go for the sale, by going for consent and then broadening consent she was able to sell a very high-ticket item.

Feel good about the fact that it's far easier to gain consent than to gain someone's hard-earned money.

Mono . . . Meet Dia

Traditional marketing has always been a monologue. One person does all the writing; the other does all the reading. Or one talks while another listens. It's always a one-way conversation, and those things rarely lead to toasty relationships.

> Traditional marketing has always been a monologue.

That's precisely why guerrilla marketing is a give and take of information. One person asks, another answers. A dialogue ensues. In time, it leads to a relationship. Score one point for dialogues. Score no points for monologues. That's one of the reasons guerrillas are so attracted to the web. It's a relationship breeding ground. They transform all their messages into dialogues, learning more about the customer-to-be and becoming better able to solve another's problems or capitalize on his own strengths.

Do this by allowing people to register for your free reports that you'll send with a one-on-one letter, your newsletter, your e-book, an article about you, or an article about them and invite contact. Make it easy. You're not going to have a chance to get close to everyone in the world. Get close to the ones you can.

Never treat others like consumers or members of a demographic group, but instead like valued guests, honored customers, and most of all, people. Some big successful companies require their salespeople to ask three questions of each prospect. The question must have nothing to do with business and probably should exclude politics or religion. The reason for this is that your main purpose is to start a conversation. Usually easy to do. Be sure you also have your elevator pitch, that 15-second description of what you do and how you can help the other guy. Memorize it but don't make it the focal point of your talk, unless, of course, the other guy wants you to. From little conversations, big orders grow.

> One of the reasons guerrillas are so attracted to the web is that it's a relationship breeding ground.

Speak Softly but Carry 200 Big Sticks

From the beginning of social interaction, there have been countless unexploited avenues of marketing—unexploited because society had other priorities. Your ancestors, if they were entrepreneurial cavemen, probably marketed their tools or nuts or berries or arrows with vigor. But they were shorthanded in the marketing weapon department.

Today, guerrillas have 200 marketing weapons that can help make up a mighty formidable arsenal. We list them for you in Chapter 12. Your competitors are probably using five or ten. For the past 20 years, we've only been listing 100. But hey, you're starting up with guerrilla marketing, and we want to give you a running start. We'll do that with 200 weapons from which you may choose, experiment, and combine. More than 100 of the weapons are absolutely free. All 200 are categorized to make it easy for you to mix and match.

Become familiar with every one of these weapons. Know what they can and can't do. Don't dare overlook even one, such as an autoresponder, that sounds complex but is simple and can quadruple your profits.

> A guerrilla marketing campaign is blend of strategy and tactics, attitudes, and company attributes.

A guerrilla marketing campaign is blend of strategy and tactics, attitudes, and company attributes. Now, you can add 200 weapons to that blend. But first do a bit of homework so that your aim will be true and your weapons will make friends of strangers.

THE 20 DIFFERENCES BETWEEN TRADITIONAL AND GUERRILLA MARKETING

1. Instead of investing money in the marketing process, you invest time, energy, imagination, and information.

2. Instead of using guesswork in your marketing, you use the science of psychology, actual laws of human behavior.

3. Instead of concentrating on traffic, responses, or gross sales, profits are the only yardstick by which you measure your marketing.

4. Instead of being oriented to companies with limitless bank accounts, guerrilla marketing is geared to small business.

5. Instead of ignoring customers once they've purchased, you have a fervent devotion to customer follow-up.

6. Instead of intimidating small business owners, guerrilla marketing removes the mystique from the entire marketing process and clarifies it.

7. Instead of competing with other businesses, guerrilla marketing preaches the gospel of cooperation, urging you to help others and let them help you.

8. Instead of trying to make sales, guerrilla marketers are dedicated to making relationships, for long-term relationships are paramount in the new millennium.

9. Instead of believing that single marketing weapons such as advertising or a web site work, guerrillas know that only marketing combinations work.

10. Instead of relying on a logo, guerrilla marketing harness the power of memes to convey entire ideas and break through the advertising clutter.

11. Instead of growing large and diversifying, guerrillas grow profitably and then maintain their focus, not an easy thing to do.

12. Instead of aiming messages at large groups, guerrilla marketing is aimed at individuals and small groups (nanocasting).

13. Instead of being unintentional by identifying only mass marketing, guerrilla marketing is always intentional, embracing even such details as how your telephone is answered.

14. Instead of growing linearly by adding new customers, guerrillas grow geometrically by enlarging the size of each transaction, generating more repeat sales, leaning upon the enormous referral power of customers, and adding new customers.

15. Instead of thinking of what a business can take, guerrilla marketing asks that you think of what a business can give in the way of free information to help customers and prospects.

16. Instead of ignoring technology in marketing, guerrilla marketing encourages you to be technocozy.

17. Instead of being "me" marketing and talking about a business, guerrilla marketing is "you" marketing and talking about the prospect.

18. Instead of attempting to make a sale with marketing, guerrilla marketing attempts to gain consent with marketing, then broadens that consent to market only to interested people.

19. Instead of a one-way monologue, guerrilla marketing promotes customer interaction with a two-way dialogue.

20. Instead of encouraging you to advertise, guerrilla marketing provides you with 200 different marketing weapons; advertising is only one of them.

9

THE RESEARCH YOU MUST DO

The Nestle Corporation in Geneva, Switzerland, asked Leo Burnett Advertising in Chicago, Illinois, where creativity came from. The answer was revealed by asking the same question to artists, dancers, writers, musicians, poets, engineers, and architects. All gave the same answer to the question. They said that creativity comes from knowledge. The more knowledge you have, the more creative you can be. Applying creativity to the arts listed above has the purpose of human enjoyment. Applying creativity to your business has the primary purpose of generating profits. If it doesn't generate profits, it's not creative.

Don't ever go down the garden path of beauty and creative expression in marketing. Sure, it's a plus if your audio and visual materials look and sound great. But that's not their job. Generating profits is their

> Applying creativity to your business has the primary purpose of generating profits. If it doesn't generate profits, it's not creative.

job. Get your artistic kicks in the concert hall. There's no place for them in the boardroom.

The Knowledge You Need

Direct your creativity towards the accumulation of knowledge you need. The path to that knowledge is illuminated by research, the start-up point for the start-up guerrilla. You're doing a good job of it now as you're immersing yourself in the basic training for a guerrilla. That training as well as your own adventures as a guerrilla marketer starts with information you've really got to have. Much of it is published on the internet. Lots of it is yours for free at your local chamber of commerce. Bookstores and libraries are bulging with just the information you need, and professional associations and groups will share it with you. Our favorite is the University of Google.

> The path to that knowledge is illuminated by research.

There's only one thing that accessible information lacks—specific information about your customers. It's laden with data about groups, but as a guerrilla, you're more interested in data about individuals. The best way to get that data is to get it yourself. Do your own research. Prepare customer and prospect questionnaires (a different one for each group) that ask a lot of questions. Have a notation at the top of the questionnaire that you're sorry to ask so many questions, but the more you know about them, the better service you can be to them.

Ask questions with answers that open new doors, such as what is your favorite sport? Favorite rock group? Favorite baseball team? Do you have a hobby? Do you have any pets? The answers to these questions can help you add immense power to your e-mail and web site. There is an old proverb: "It is better to know something specific about your spouse than know everything about marriage." The same holds true for buyer-seller relationships. The "something specific" is what you get with research and the way to switch a start-up marketing campaign into a higher gear.

If you want a place to exercise your creativity, it's in your customer questionnaire. Most business owners know most of the right answers. Guerrilla business owners also know most of the right questions. Knowing the right questions to ask and then asking them is one of the arts of the start-up guerrilla marketing campaign.

Processing what you learn is what it's all about because that's where the action begins taking place. You notice a great number of customers in three zip codes. That spurs a mailing to those codes. You must be doing or saying something right. What can it be?

Naturally, a guerrilla's view of research begins with research into his own customers. Important as they are, there are still many other areas deserving of further exploration. First on that list are your prospects, those people who for some silly reason haven't yet purchased from you. Hey! Hold on a second. Maybe it wasn't a silly reason. Maybe it was you doing a silly thing or missing an important detail in customer service. Always look at it like this: If your prospects aren't your customers, there's got to be a reason. Find out what that reason it and then correct it. Be relentless. Be pig-headed and single-purposed, but do everything you can do to transform all of your prospects into customers. That may not happen exactly. But your efforts won't go unrewarded. My boss and idol Leo Burnett said, "When you reach for the stars, you might not get one, but you're not likely to come up with a handful of mud either."

> There is an old proverb: "It is better to know something specific about your spouse than know everything about marriage."

What Are People Really Buying?

They are buying for a variety of different reasons—18 in fact.

1. Solutions to their problems
2. Freedom from pain
3. Promises you make (So make them carefully)
4. Wealth, safety, success, security, love, and acceptance
5. Your guarantee, reputation, and good name
6. Other people's opinions of your business

7. Believable claims, not simply honest claims
8. Brand names over strange names
9. Easy access to information offered by your web site
10. The consistency they've seen you exhibit
11. The stature of the media in which you market
12. The professionalism of your marketing materials
13. Value, which is not the same as price
14. Freedom from risk, granted by your warranty
15. Convenience in purchasing
16. Neatness (and assume that's how you do business)
17. Honesty (One dishonest word means no sale)
18. Speedy delivery

They aren't buying for the reasons some marketers think. They don't buy for:

- Fancy adjectives,
- Exaggerated claims,
- Clever headlines,
- Special effects,
- Marketing that screams, or
- Marketing that even hints at amateurishness.

Why People Buy

You may think you know why your customers buy from you, but there's a good chance they buy for reasons other than the reasons you think. People seek a wide array of benefits when they're in a buying mindset. If you are communicating any one of those benefits to the people who want them this very instant, you've virtually made the sale.

People do not buy because marketing is clever, but because marketing strikes a responsive chord in their minds, and its resonance makes them want the advantages of what you are selling. Your customers do not buy because they're being marketed to or sold to.

Instead, they buy because you help them realize the merits of owning what you offer.

If you already know why people buy, do you know *all* the reasons? The more of those reasons you know, the better you'll be able to market. Geoff Ayling, in his superb book, *Rapid Response Advertising* (Business & Professional Publishing, 1999), provides wannabe guerrillas with a full 50 reasons why people buy. There are really far more than 50, but we have a feeling that these 50 will get your creative juices flowing. People make purchases for these, among many reasons:

1. To make more money—even though it can't buy happiness
2. To become more comfortable, even a bit more
3. To attract praise—because almost everybody loves it
4. To increase enjoyment—of life, of business, of virtually anything
5. To possess things of beauty—because they nourish the soul
6. To avoid criticism—which nobody wants
7. To make their work easier – a constant need to many people
8. To speed up their work—because people know that time is precious
9. To keep up with the Joneses—there are Joneses in everybody's lives
10. To feel opulent—a rare, but valid reason to make a purchase
11. To look younger—due to the reverence placed upon youthfulness
12. To become more efficient—because efficiency saves time
13. To buy friendship—we didn't know it's for sale, but it often is
14. To avoid effort—because nobody loves to work too hard
15. To escape or avoid pain—which is an easy path to making a sale
16. To protect their possessions—because they worked hard to get them
17. To be in style—because few people enjoy being out of style
18. To avoid trouble—because trouble is never a joy

19. To access opportunities—because they open the doors to good things

20. To express love—one of the noblest reasons to make any purchase

21. To be entertained—because entertainment is usually fun

22. To be organized—because order makes lives simpler

23. To feel safe—because security is a basic human need

24. To conserve energy—their own or their planet's sources of energy

25. To be accepted—because that means security as well as love

26. To save time—because they know time is more valuable than money

27. To become more fit and healthy—seems to me that's an easy sale

28. To attract the opposite sex—never underestimate the power of love

29. To protect their family—tapping into another basic human need

30. To emulate others—because the world is teeming with role models

31. To protect their reputation—because they worked hard to build it

32. To feel superior—which is why status symbols are sought after

33. To be trendy—because they know their friends will notice

34. To be excited—because people need excitement in a humdrum life

35. To communicate better — because they want to be understood

36. To preserve the environment—giving rise to cause-related marketing

37. To satisfy an impulse—a basic reason behind a multitude of purchases

38. To save money—the most important reason to 14 percent of the population

39. To be cleaner—because unclean often goes with unhealthy and unloved
40. To be popular—because inclusion beats exclusion every time
41. To gratify curiosity — it kills the cat but motivates the sale
42. To satisfy their appetite—because hunger is not a good thing
43. To be individual—because all of us are, and some of us need assurance
44. To escape stress—need we explain?
45. To gain convenience—because simplicity makes life easier
46. To be informed—because it's no joy to be perceived as ignorant
47. To give to others—another way you can nourish your soul
48. To feel younger—because that equates with vitality and energy
49. To pursue a hobby—because all work and no play, etc.
50. To leave a legacy—because that's a way to live forever

We must add one more area about which you should be creative, one more reason that motivates people to make a purchase, and that area deals with pain. Thomas Jefferson said, "The art of life is the art of avoiding pain; and he is the best pilot, who steers clearest of the rocks and shoals with which it is beset." More recently, Sam Deep and Lyle Sussman, who wrote *Close the Deal* (Perseus Books Group, 1998), teach the importance of pain and the ways to learn where it resides. If you know exactly, you've got a heckuva great starting point for your creativity.

Now that you've got 51 ways to win the hearts and business of your prospects, we think you'll have an easier job of winning sales and profits.

Successful Marketing

The best marketing *builds confidence* and *invites a purchase*. Best and most unique of all, the best marketing gets through to people. That's why knowing a lot about your prospects will help you stand apart from your competitors and shine in the minds of your prospects and customers.

Once you've learned all you can about your customers and your prospects, what's the next area worth researching? A smart place to focus is your own industry. Research that industry—how did the world functioned before Google?—and get a feel for what the winners are doing, the latest trends, and for signs of any competitors you might have.

Market Domination

One of the secrets to market domination is knocking yourself off. NOT cloning yourself, but creating a new unique selling proposition in the same market.

That's why Toyota created Lexus. It's why McDonalds started Chipotle. It's not just big companies either; it's just as true with "little" guys on the internet. In some of the most competitive markets imaginable, you see 11 real ads on the first page, and most people don't know that two parent companies might be responsible for five or six of them.

Hey, if you've successfully gained a foothold in one market—and you understand that market deeply—and want to grow your business why go to the trouble of learning a brand-new niche? Do something in the one you're already in. Create a new offer that's so appealing, it takes its place along with the other top dogs: New product, new web site, new Google account.

Don't ever forget that on the *any* search term there's a whole spectrum of tastes and desires that the keyword represents. One web site and one ad can only cater to a handful of them. There are still others you're not serving. But you can.

As lush and fascinating as the internet may be for research, we can't help but point you in the direction of trade shows where you'll not only get a state-of-the-moment feel for your industry but you'll also get a lot of inside information not yet published online. The networking at these shows may be more valuable than anything on the trade show floor.

The product or service you offer also merits abundant research time. The better you know your offering, the better equipped you'll be to talk about it, understand it, market it. Eventually, you'll be called upon to prepare a benefits list, that actual in-writing list of the benefits people gain by buying from you. We urge you to put a lot of effort and creativity into this list because it's what you'll be communicating to your prospects and customers. They'll then make their decision to purchase (or not to purchase) based upon the benefits you do (or don't) convey.

Your next point of research will be your competition, which you'll already know pretty well because of your forays into studying your industry and your product. Learn what they say and where they say it. Maintain vigil here because they'll tip their hand frequently by how they adjust their message and their media. You don't want to copy them but you do want to be aware of what they're up to. You can be sure that they're checking up on you. You might even buy the product of the leader in your industry. Get to see firsthand its sales presentation, display, packaging, follow-up, and product itself. Learning from leaders is a guerrilla strength.

Don't fail to research life outside your own industry. Get to know the media, online and offline available to you. Get to know the internet on an intimate basis within your industry. Start-up guerrillas engage in a monthly half-hour surf of the internet to catch the best that's online—in and out of their industry. The research you put in looking for media opportunities for your company will pay off every time.

That research should include researching the latest technology that might empower your business. The move in entrepreneurship is toward automation. Happily, automation is not expensive. Your company can give off the vibes of a huge, lavishly funded corporation with a constantly busy staff, when the truth is it's just little old you pushing the right button on your automated customer profitability center. Technology can help you in the areas of marketing, production, finances, distribution, and a whole lot more. Skip it if you don't need it, but don't miss it if it can contribute to your profitability. It probably can. More people earn money while they sleep than ever before.

Because you are starting up your guerrilla marketing program, we didn't explore a totally different kind of research, one that we applaud and respect. But assuming you aren't yet a wealthy and thriving company, we nudge you in the direction of free research, which is what we described in this chapter. Later, when you've taken our advice and are a wealthy and thriving company, we'll suggest that you look into paid research, which takes over the entire research function, from asking the right questions to analyzing the answers. The right question can be the making of a company.

RESEARCH

- your customers
- your prospects
- your industry
- outside your industry
- your product or service
- the latest industry technology
- your competition

How to Research Your Competitors

The first step in launching a successful guerrilla marketing attack is to find out exactly how your business stacks up with your competition. This is commonly referred to as doing research. In guerrilla terms this is called "spying." Guerrillas find out all they can by spying on their competitors, their industry, and especially, themselves. Here's some ways to snazz up your snooping:

1. *Order something*. Buy something from yourself. Buy something from some of your competitors. Do it by phone, mail, or in person. Keep an eagle eye for the smoothness or rough edges in their entire process and your own. Note especially when they do their follow-up. See what you can learn to improve your own business.

2. *Visit your competitors*. You or your trusted "co-spy" should visit your place as a customer might, and then visit the premises of your competitors. Visit their web sites and take notes on every

CHECK IN ON YOUR SELF

There was once a little boy who walked into a store and ask the proprietor if he could use his phone. "Why certainly" he replied.

The little boy dialed a number and said to the person on the other end, " I'm calling you to offer you the services of the best yard boy in town."

"Well, to tell you the truth," the person at the other end responded, "We feel we already have the best yard boy in town."

The little boy then said, "I really called because I want you to have the most beautiful yard on your street, and I want you to feel a sense of pride when you see it."

"I must say," was the response, "We do feel a sense of pride whenever we look at our lawn."

"Well if that's the case," said the little boy, "congratulations, I'm really happy for you." He then hung up the phone and handed it back to the store owner.

"Young man," the owner exclaimed, "I couldn't help but overhear your conversation, and I must say, with an attitude like that, you'll have no trouble getting a job one day as a yard boy."

"Oh, I'm already a yard boy" the little boy proclaimed. "In fact, I'm the yard boy for the people I just called. I was just checking up on myself!"

single detail that is better than yours. Note the little details that win or lose prospects.

3. *Phone your competitors.* Focus on the personality and attitude of the person who answers the phone. If it's warmer and friendlier than the person who answers your phone, teach your phone answerer how to do it.

4. *Request something.* Ask for a price list or a brochure. See how your request is fulfilled, concentrating on speed and follow-up. Do you handle requests as professionally as your competition?

5. *Compare everything.* Look through the eyes of your prospect and compare your and your competitors' service, pricing, packaging, people, selection, follow-up, signs, quality, delivery, and attitude. Guerrillas know they compete in many arenas and must be the superior entry at all times.

6. *Buy something.* It always helps you to own the product or use the service of your competitors, because owning is the essence of down-and-dirty. If your competition is a public company, buy a share of stock so that you can spy by means of its annual report and shareholder meeting.

7. *Spy on yourself.* Spying enables you to spot your own deficiencies as well as your own advantages.

10

WRITING A BENEFITS LIST

As we hope you already know, people do not care about your company, but they care like crazy about themselves. That's why the words you use must be about them and not about you. Companies that have thought things through realize that those benefits should also be about the prospect and not about the company. So although we enthusiastically recommend that you create a benefits list, we hope you realize that it is about benefits that people get when they buy your product more than it is about benefits that you offer. That little distinction makes a big difference.

The Benefits List Meeting

A good benefits list begins with a meeting. The meeting should be attended by you, your employees, your top associates, fushion marketing partner,

A good benefits
list begins with
a meeting. The
meeting should
be attended by
you, your top
associates, your
marketing team,
and at least one
customer.

and at least one customer. The reason to invite customers is because they may be aware of important benefits that have escaped your attention.

While compiling that list, it's very important to be as immodest as you've ever been before. A benefits list meeting is no place for modesty or shyness. It's a concert hall devoted to you tooting your own horn. The more benefits you can put onto that list, the easier you will make it for the people who design and write your web site, your marketing materials, your signs, your e-mails.

They are the sharpshooters. You are the ammunition makers. Your ammunition, designed not to hurt but to help, are benefits that people derive by purchasing from you.

Your Competitive Advantage

Once you've completed a benefits list, take the time to draw a circle around any benefits you offer that are not offered by your competitors. Those are your competitive advantages. Those are most likely going

CARROT INCENTIVE

A bookstore had a benefits list meeting at which the customer attending was asked this question: "You live five miles away from our store and there are four bookstores between you and us. So why do you patronize our bookstore?" The customer shot back the answer, "Your carrot cake. It's the best in the county!"

The bookseller's benefits list probably included good lighting, an expanded selection, convenient hours, a personable and well-trained staff, author readings every Friday, live music every Sunday evening, and free shipping. But it certainly didn't say anything about carrot cake. Only with a customer in attendance would that idea even have come up. That's why you invite at least one customer to your benefits list meeting.

YOUR PLACE OR MINE?

When an automotive detailer opened for business in the county where we lived, he sent us a card asking "Your place or mine?" We called him in response to his card and asked what he meant by his question. He said that there were so many detailers competing with him that he and his partner decided to give customers a choice: have their cars detailed at their garage or at their customer's home or office. He said that his service was doing very well.

We weren't at all surprised because he was the only one offering the "your place or mine?" approach. It was a competitive advantage that worked exceptionally well for him. The most amazing thing is that he didn't go into business with that advantage. He had to invent it to deal with all of the competitors offering the same service.

to be the benefits where you hang your marketing hat. What if you don't have a competitive advantage? You create one. You invent one. Then you live up to it.

The Benefits of Your Product or Service

As soon as you clearly determine what your target market wants, you can orchestrate a marketing campaign based on addressing those needs.

What do people really want? To be:

- Happy
- Safe
- Successful
- Wealthy
- Liked
- Loved

They also want to:

> Draw a circle around any benefits you offer that are not offered by your competitors. Those are your competitive advantages.

- Have a sense of purpose
- Have fun
- Be pain free
- Eat tasty foods

Marketers often confuse features with benefits. It's important to differentiate between them. *Features* are the things inherent in your product or service. *Benefits* are what the buyer gets from your product or service. The following examples will help clarify the distinction between the two.

- *Driver airbags.* Feelings of safety and security
- *Ergonomic chair.* Relieves pressure on spine, stress-relief
- *Telecoaching.* No commute, accept calls from anywhere
- *Drill bit.* Creates holes easily to help you complete your project.

Take a few minutes to write out the most unique and desirable benefits you offer your target market.

Tune into their favorite radio station: WIIFM- What's In It For Me?

The goal is not to list a lot of benefits, but to find the ones that will meet the desires of your customers. Answer questions such as:

- "What do they really want?"
- "How am I different?"
- "What do I offer that my competition doesn't?"

Return to your list and place an asterisk (*) next to the benefit that you feel is your most important competitive advantage.

In the future, you may have to hire a professional guerrilla marketer or copywriter to help you craft winning web copy. What do you tell that hired gun? You simply hand him your benefits list so she knows where to start. If you have a couple of competitive advantages circled, that's even better. She'll have an even better handle on what to say in your marketing copy.

Naturally, the time to make your benefits list is right at the outset, before you publish anything about your business. You don't want to forget the important things. You don't want to leave anything out. You do know where you want to aim your brightest lights. Any business owner who wants to be success-bound starts out with a benefits list—one of the starting points for a guerrilla marketing campaign.

The cost of compiling a benefits list is nil. And yet, you'll be asked to create copy on the spot for the Yellow Pages, for a program for a local event, for a high school fundraiser. What will you say in your copy? Don't risk forgetting your most important benefits. Don't take the chance of leaving out something important. Just use your benefits list to nourish your mind and ignite your memory cells. You might be offering several benefits with which you can win customers for life.

That's why you might consider including all of your benefits on your web site. You never know which button will be the hot button for your prospects. You never know which benefit will win business for you from your competitors. You never know which competitive advantage is the one that did the trick to win a good, steady customer. But you will know if you start with a benefits list.

11

DEVELOPING
A MEME

"**M**eme" is a relatively new word, having been coined in 1976 by Richard Dawkins in Oxford, England. You've seen memes almost all your life, but you perhaps didn't know what they were called. They influenced your behavior, communicated clearly to you, and didn't use language to do it. Immediately you knew what they wanted of you and most of the time, you did it.

The most common memes in the world, apart from the wheel, are international traffic symbols. A logo communicates the name of a company. That's not enough for a company starting up with a high-powered guerrilla marketing campaign. That kind of company now uses a meme, which communicates an entire idea. And in this day of too much marketing clutter—the average person is exposed to 3,700 marketing messages each day—a meme breaks through that clutter, saves money for you, saves time for your prospects, and helps you earn serious profits.

You see a person at the edge of the road holding out his thumb. That's a meme communicating the idea, "I need a lift." You're driving and someone blinks his lights at you. That's another meme saying, "Hey, dim your bright high-beam headlights." Immediately you know exactly what a meme is about.

And that's why guerrilla marketers in droves are creating memes for their company. A simple swoosh might be enough for Nike, but because it's not a meme and fails to communicate an idea, it's only a logo, and that means it goes only halfway.

When early man saw a wagon on wheels enter its territory, no instructions were needed. Instantly, everyone knew what was happening and how wheels work. Sure, they carried goods from place to place, but because memes are viral and are very capable of spreading, a wheel also carries the idea of a meme from mind to mind.

The world is loaded with memes such as the cross, a flag, an Energizer Bunny who just keeps on going. The Michelin Man is a meme. He conveys comfort and softness and tires and is the meme for a tire company. The Green Giant conveys the meme of healthy foods grown by a big, happy giant. The Pillsbury Doughboy is a meme reminding you that baking can be easy and it can also be fun. Your task is create your own meme, plant an idea in the minds of your public.

A meme is recognized as the lowest common denominator of an idea. It is a basic unit of communicaton. A meme actually alters human behavior, and motivates people. It is simplicity itself and is understandable in seconds—or even faster. A meme can be graphic, such as the hitchhiker; verbal, ala "Lean Cuisine"; or action, such as pouring Gatorade over the head of the winning coach in the Super Bowl.

You want your meme to work everywhere: on television, on signs, on a web site, on your business card, in the Yellow Pages, everywhere you're communicating with your target audience as well as with the entire world.

It's astonishingly simple to create a meme. Simply study your benefits list and focus upon those that are visual. Some of those

> The average person is exposed to 3,700 marketing messages each day–a meme breaks through that clutter.

> A meme is recognized as the lowest common denominator of an idea. It is a basic unit of communicaton. A meme actually alters human behavior, and motivates people.

MEMES: THE NEWEST AND MOST POTENT MARKETING WEAPON

1. Lowest common demoninator of an idea

2. A basic unit of communication

3. Alters human behavior and movitates people

4. Simplicity itself; understandable in seconds

5. Graphic, words, or action

communicate both a benefit you offer and an idea. Simplify that visual, then start using it in place of your logo, if indeed, you did have a logo.

One of the most powerful and ancient memes in history was the wheel. A wagon with spoked wheels carries not only freight from place to place; it also carries the unmistakable idea of a wagon with spoked wheels from mind to mind. Many other non-marketing memes have made their way into our culture.

The hula hoop, snowboarding, rollerblading, miniskirts, Beatle haircuts, bottled water—a long list of concepts such as these seem to roar through the community like a brush fire.

Even the word "God" is a meme because it reduces the enormous idea down to a single word, which represents the entire concept of belief in a supreme being. The folowing will help you understand memes better.

How Memes Compare with Beliefs

- *Beliefs are feelings of certainty about what something means.* Memes are sources of information, which created that feeling of certainty.

- *Beliefs are effects.* Memes are causes.
- *Beliefs are attitudes that spring from ideas.* Memes are simplified representations of ideas.
- *Beliefs are feelings or inclinations.* Memes are basically icons with an implied subtext.
- *Beliefs are internal.* Memes are external until they replicate. When they do, they become internalized and develop into beliefs.
- *Beliefs can last a lifetime and might take a while to enter a mind.* Memes invade the mind in an instant and don't necessarily last a lifetime. In marketing, however, they ought to be created to last a lifetime.
- *Beliefs are expanded attitudes about life.* Memes are compressed and transmissible packets of information.
- *Beliefs usually take a while to grasp entirely.* Memes are the quickest and most effective ways to transmit and receive complex concepts from one mind to another.
- *Beliefs require conscious consideration.* Memes are transmitted in a second.

All but one of the most famous memes were around long before Dawkins coined the word "meme." Each one represents an entire idea. Memes are always ideas, but ideas are not always memes. But if the ideas are distilled, compressed, simplified, and focused, and then presented in a manner that can be communicated through a wide range of media—from the internet to a billboard—they might become memes.

But not all great ideas or even great marketing campaigns furnish us with a meme. To see this up close and personal, study the top ten slogans of the past century, again selected by *Advertising Age*. Some have memes. Some do not. Those with memes tell us about the product being marketing. Those without memes tell us nothing about the product or its benefits.

The top ten slogans of the 20th century are:

1. *Diamonds are forever* (DeBeers): These three words are a meme.

THE BEST KNOWN MEMES OF THE 20TH CENTURY

The Marlboro Man: Marlboro cigarettes

Ronald McDonald: McDonald's restaurants

The Green Giant: Green Giant vegetables

Betty Crocker: Betty Crocker food products

The Energizer Bunny: Eveready Energizer batteries

The Pillsbury Doughboy: Assorted Pillsbury foods

Aunt Jemima: Aunt Jemima pancake mixes and syrup

The Michelin Man: Michelin tires

Tony the Tiger: Kellogg's Frosted Flakes

Elsie the Cow: Borden dairy products

2. *Just do it* (Nike): No meme here, just three words.

3. *The pause that refreshes* (Coca-Cola): Definitely a meme.

4. *Tastes great, less filling* (Miller Lite): A meme without question.

5. *We try harder* (Avis): A meme telling us about the company.

6. *Good to the last drop* (Maxwell House): A meme about the product.

7. *Breakfast of champions* (Wheaties): Another meme about the product.

8. *Does she . . . or doesn't she?* (Clairol): A meme at work.

9. *When it rains it pours* (Morton Salt): A meme with a visual.

10. *Where's the beef?* (Wendy's): A short-lived meme, if a meme at all.

To show you that social conscience rarely enters into a person's purchasing behavior, notice how that top ten memes and meme slogans include an air polluter (Avis), nutritionless sugar water (Coca-Cola), one reviled carcinogen (Marlboro), two companies infamous for shaky labor practices (DeBeers, Nike), two purveyors of savory cardiovascular time bombs (McDonald's, Wendy's), one booze peddler (Miller Lite), one product that is laced with caffeine (Maxwell House), and one cosmetic product preying on vanity (Clairol). Fortunately, cause-related marketing is coming to the fore.

To get your meme consciousness into even higher gear, consider the slogans selected for honorable mention.

- *Look Ma, no cavities!* (Crest toothpaste): Meme about product.
- *Let your fingers do the walking* (Yellow Pages): Meme with visual.
- *Loose lips sink ships* (public service): Meme with visual.
- *M&Ms melt in your mouth, not in your hand* (M&M candies): Meme
- *We bring good things to life* (General Electric): Not really a meme.

Memes travel. Memes spread. Memes are viral. In fact, in scientific circles, they're referred to as "mind viruses." Memes are simple to create. And memes can goose your company's profitability, not to mention civilization itself. For memes to become contagious, which should be the goal of those who create memes for their business, three factors are necessary:

1. *Extreme simplicity transmitting the core message.* When you see an ad for Maxell tape, you see a man listening to his sound system, his hair and tie flying as though he's facing a powerful wind. This meme communicates that something powerful is coming from his sound system. Then Maxell lets readers know it's the quality of the recording tape.
2. *Emotional impact so that people feel the message internally.* In the previous chapter, we explored the power of emotions in marketing. You see a commercial showing a woman being given a gift by her guy and her eyes mist up. Then, you hear the line, "A diamond is forever." You can't help but feel the tug on your heartstrings. Score one point for De Beers.
3. *Critical mass so that enough people are exposed to spread it.* How many people is enough to constitute critical mass? It depends upon the product being marketed. But rather than looking for

a number, look instead for a trend. If the number of people using your offering continues to grow, you may be heading toward critical mass. Hotmail grew a subscriber base more rapidly than any company in the history of the world—faster than any new online, internet, or print publication ever. Today, Hotmail is the largest e-mail provider in the world. In its first one-and-a-half years, thanks to viral marketing helping them achieve critical mass, Hotmail signed up more than 12 million subscribers. Yet from company launch to 12 million users—now 30 million—Hotmail spent less than $500,000 on marketing, advertising, and promotion. This compares to the $20 million plus spent on advertising and brand promotion by Juno, Hotmail's closest competitor with but a fraction of its users. The marketing meme used by Hotmail: "Get your free e-mail at Hotmail." That's it. How simple can you get?

Nonmarketing Memes

Although there are several memes that have been used in marketing—such as Elsie the Cow for Borden's, an arm and a hammer for Arm and Hammer Baking Soda, Camel cigarettes' Joe Camel, MGM's lion, Paramount's mountain, Columbia's woman standing with a torch, Smokey the Bear for fire prevention, and McGruff the Crime Dog for crime prevention—most memes have little to do with marketing, which is a shame since they convey their ideas instantly.

Everyone knows many nonmarketing memes:

- The outstretched thumb of a hitchhiker.
- The thumbs-up sign for positivity.
- The middle finger for negativity.
- Three fingers representing the Boy Scouts of America.
- The fish for Christianity.
- Flashing headlights to indicate "your brights are on!" or "police ahead."

- The dove and the olive branch to signify peace.
- The blindfolded woman holding scales to indicate justice.
- The caduceus wand to symbolize medicine.
- The rainbow to symbolize Hawaii, homosexuality, and the rainbow coalition.
- The anchor to signify a sailor.
- The flamingo to signify Florida.
- The eagle for the United States.
- Purple for royalty.
- A pink triangle for gay and lesbian causes.
- And let's not forgets: "Is that your final answer?"

All of these examples show that memes can take many forms and stand for many causes unrelated to marketing.

MUSICAL MEMES

Memes can be musical as well as visual or verbal, as proven by these jingles selected as the top ten of the 20th century:

1. *You deserve a break today* (McDonalds).
2. *Be all that you can be* (U.S. Army).
3. *Pepsi Cola hits the spot* (Pepsi Cola).
4. *M'mmm, M'mmm good* (Campbell's).
5. *See the USA in your Chevrolet* (GM).
6. *I wish I were an Oscar Meyer Wiener* (Oscar Meyer).
7. *Double your pleasure, double your fun* (Wrigley's Doublemint gum).
8. *Winston tastes good like a cigarette should* (Winston).
9. *It's the real thing* (Coca-Cola).
10. *A little dab'll do ya* (Brylcreem).

A Radar for Memes

A good exercise for guerrillas who wish to develop a meme for their company is to develop a radar for existing memes. Surf the net, scan a magazine, and view commercials with an eye towards spotting memes. Once you find one, think backward from the meme to the thought process that generated it. You see an illustration of an elderly man with a small beard and a big smile. Immediately, you recognize him as Colonel Sanders. How do you suppose the company came up with that meme? It's pretty easy to tell, just by considering the name of the company and the guy who mixed all those herbs and spices to create his chicken recipe. No heavy thinking necessary.

Practice by looking at the following italicized memes and seeing if you can figure out how the company got the meme.

- *"Have a Coke and a smile."* One of many memes used by Coca-Cola over the years and one of the few that mentions Coke's name.
- *"There's a Ford in your future."* It was used for a long time by the Ford Motor Company, as if you didn't know.
- *"We do chicken right."* This was for KFC and didn't mention its name but did mention its primary product. "Finger-lickin' good" was one of its early memes, and for the life of me, I can't see why it was dropped.
- *"How do your spell 'relief?' R-O-L-A-I-D-S."* It gives a benefit and mentions the name of the marketer.
- *"Mmmm, good . . . Mmmm, good . . . that's what Campbell Soups are . . . Mmmm, Mmmm, good!"* It states a benefit, mentions the name, and works well with music.
- *"Schaefer is the one beer to have when you're having more than one."* This is a meme directed to beer lovers rather than mere beer dilatantes.
- *"I wish I were an Oscar Meyer weiner."* It conveys the fun of Oscar Meyer hot dogs as well as their name.

- *"Winston tastes good like a cigarette should."* This meme kept Winston among the leaders until the Marlboro man knocked it from its perch.

Off-the-Mark Memes

Not all, or even most, projected memes work. Let's examine some memes that were off the mark, primarily because they didn't mention the name of the product and could have been for anyone:

- *"I can't believe I ate the whole thing,"* generated a lot of laughs for Alka-Seltzer, but didn't generate any profits. Somebody hits the bullseye on the wrong target.
- *"Does she or doesn't she?"* was a famous and successful verbal meme even though it didn't mention Clairol. Still, a lot of women were motivated by the line to purchase L'Oreal.
- *"America's most gifted whiskey,"* was cute and clever for Four Roses, but it could apply to a host of booze brands.
- *"We bring good things to life,"* is for General Electric but could be for many other companies as well. GE spends a fortune reminding you that they are doing the talking, but guerrillas rarely have a fortune to waste on such a vague meme.
- *"Getting there is half the fun,"* was a truism marketed by Cunard Cruises but might have been a truism for lots of other companies, too.
- *"Quality is Job #1"* was used to juxtaposition with the Ford logo, so people knew who was talking. But as a stand-alone meme, it is too anonymous.

Those examples prove that the evolution of memes could not get started until evolution had paved the way by creating a species—homo sapiens—with brains that could provide shelter and habits of communication that could provide transmission conduits for memes. Those conduits are now called "the media."

The Hallmark of Guerrilla Creativity

A powerful meme is the hallmark of guerrilla creativity. It implants an idea in the minds of your prospects. And it reduces the cost of your marketing because you don't have to spend so much educating people. So when you come up with a meme for your own company, learn to cherish it and dismiss all thoughts of abandoning it.

The longer you use a meme, the stronger it gets. So the idea is to create yours, then start using it as soon as you can. It can be large or small. It can use color or be in simple black and white. Just be sure that when people see it, they know the idea you're trying to convey. In *Guerrilla Creativity* (Houghton Mifflin, 2001), we wrote an entire book about using memes in marketing, but now you know all you have to know in order to create a meme that can contribute to your profits for a long time.

How long has Rice Krispies been showing the characters Snap, Crackle, and Pop? How long has a cowboy been a symbol of Marlboros and Marlboro Country? A meme has a long life and can make a mighty contribution to the beauty of your bottom line.

As a person who is blessed to be inaugurating a guerrilla marketing campaign right now, take advantage of your splendid timing!

FAMILIARITY IS THE KEY

We remember when people were terrified of the word "internet" because it was a new word. Now, everybody knows what the internet is, what it does, and how it can make your company more profitable. The same thing is happening with the word, "meme." True, it's a new word. But, within a few years, all marketers will know what it is, many will proudly display it on all their marketing materials, and it will become as well-known as the internet.

Right now, at the start, is the best time to expose your meme to the planet. Do yourself a favor. Look at newspapers, magazines, web sites, and signs. See how many memes you can spot. There won't be many because memes were born outside the marketing world and are just coming into their own. Make yours one of the first memes in marketing. Keep it simple. Think in terms of clarity of idea rather than sheer beauty. When a person sees your meme, you don't want them saying, "What a beautiful meme!" Instead, you want them to say, "I want that product!"

12

SELECTING YOUR GUERRILLA MARKETING WEAPONS

If the guerrilla marketing strategy is the brains of a marketing program, the guerrilla marketing weapons are the muscles. You certainly won't need all the weapons about to be suggested here, but you also cannot remain oblivious to any of them. Times change. A guerrilla marketing attack is a 360-degree assault.

As one who is just starting with his guerrilla marketing campaign, you'll find this is unquestionably the best time to learn about the weapons, about their plentitude, their potency, and their economy. For us, just having you know the range of your selection lets us breathe deeply. Two hundred weapons, 200 choices, countless combinations.

You can't help but be aware of your relationship with each of the weapons as you read its name. Either you know it intimately and are expert in its usage, you've tried it and may still be using it but know in

> As the guerrilla marketing strategy is the brains of a marketing program, the guerrilla marketing weapons are the muscles.

your heart that your expertise is limited, you've never tried it, or you know what it's about but don't feel that it's the ticket for you at this junction. Nowhere is it written that you must use all 200 weapons. Hall of fame guerrillas have achieved marketing greatness with only a handful.

Unless you're in business for laughs over profits, you've got to become familiar with all of these 200 weapons. It's the grown-up thing to do. Guerrilla marketing is fun but it is not child's play. You should experiment with several of the 200 weapons, being ultra-careful not to waste your precious marketing investments by analyzing how well each weapon fared. If it cost more than it earned, eliminate it unless you've got a good reason not to. If it earns more than it costs, use twice as much of it next go-round. Do other weapons produce even more profits for you? Experiment and find out.

Once you've got your magic formula, it's time to ruthlessly cut all the weapons that aren't proving their worth. The phrase to remember is "lethal combinations." That's what you want. You get it by knowing all the contenders, eliminating the losers, and doubling up on the winners.

Don't worry that we're going to throw a wagonload of weapons into a pile in front of you. We've neatly categorized the weapons to make things as clear and simple as possible.

Some of the weapons fall into the category of "mini-media" because while they certainly aren't major media, they definitely are media. Enormous companies have been built with the mini-media alone. The mini-media are:

1. A marketing plan
2. A marketing calendar
3. Identity
4. Business cards
5. Stationery
6. Personal letters
7. Telephone marketing
8. A toll-free number

9. A vanity phone number
10. The Yellow Pages
11. Postcards
12. Postcard decks
13. Classified ads
14. Per-order and per-inquiry advertising
15. Free ads in shoppers
16. Circulars and fliers
17. Community bulletin boards
18. Movie ads
19. Outside signs
20. Street banners
21. A window display
22. Inside signs
23. Posters
24. Canvassing
25. Door hangers
26. An elevator pitch
27. A value story
28. Backend sales
29. Letters of recommendation
30. Attendance at trade shows

Another option for you are the maxi-media, the logical category of larger, costlier, splashier, and more traditional media. These are 19th and 20th century weapons, still effective but with lots of the luster gone. The maxi-media are:

31. Advertising
32. Direct mail
33. Newspaper ads
34. Radio spots
35. Magazine ads
36. Billboards
37. Television commercials

The newest category, the e-media, is new because most of its weapons were not even a gleam in a software engineer's eye at the time *Guerrilla Marketing* turned up in bookstores and libraries. These nonetheless merit a category of their own, and a hefty one it is. The e-media are:

38. A computer
39. A printer or fax machine
40. Chat rooms
41. Forums
42. Internet bulletin boards
43. List building
44. Personalized e-mail
45. An e-mail signature
46. Canned e-mail
47. Bulk e-mail
48. Audio and video postcards
49. A domain name
50. A web site
51. A landing page
52. A merchant account
53. A shopping cart
54. Auto-responders
55. A search engine ranking
56. Electronic brochures
57. RSS feeds
58. Blogs
59. Podcasting
60. A personal e-zine
61. Ads in other e-zines
62. E-books
63. Content provision
64. Webinars
65. Joint ventures

66. Word-of-mouse
67. Viral marketing
68. eBay and other auction sites
69. Click analyzers
70. Pay-per-click ads
71. Search engine keywords
72. Google adwords
73. Sponsored links
74. Reciprocal link exchanges
75. Banner exchanges
76. Web conversion rates

The Info-Media

Most media imparts information, but some media are all about information, rather than having it merely as a peripheral reason for their existence. Some of these media are old. Some are new. All are capable of turning a business around. And some can do that for free. The info-media are:

77. Knowledge of your market
78. Research studies
79. Specific customer data
80. Case studies
81. Sharing
82. Brochures
83. Catalogs
84. Business directories
85. Public service announcements
86. A newsletter
87. Speeches
88. Free consultations
89. Free demonstrations
90. Free seminars
91. Articles

92. Columns
93. Writing a book
94. Publishing-on-demand
95. Workshops
96. Teleseminars
97. Infomercials
98. Constant learning

The Human Media

Many media are things. Others are people. There are so many that are people that we decided to create a category of solely these media. When we say they are about people, we're really saying that they're about you. You are the one who can breathe life into some of these media and you are the one who actually is the media. These over-looked weapons of marketing are far too powerful to be overlooked. The human media are:

99. Marketing insight
100. Yourself
101. Your employees and reps
102. A designated guerrilla
103. Employee attire
104. Your social demeanor
105. Your target audience
106. Your circle of influence
107. Your contact time with customers
108. How you say "Hello" and "Goodbye"
109. Your teaching ability
110. Stories
111. Sales training
112. Use of downtime
113. Networking
114. Professional titles
115. Affiliate marketing

116. Media contacts
117. "A"-List customers
118. Your core story
119. A sense of urgency
120. Limited time or quantity offers
121. A call to action
122. Satisfied customers

The Non-Media

The previous category about human beings is indeed, about human beings. And this upcoming category, about the non-media, is definitely not about the media. The non-media can make substantial contributions to your profits, but they won't do so as standard media. Even though these suggestions are not officially "media," they should not escape your notice. In fact, I'm shining a bright light upon them with every one listed here. The non-media are:

123. A benefits list
124. Competitive advantages
125. Gifts
126. Service
127. Public relations
128. Fusion marketing
129. Barter
130. Word-of-mouth
131. Buzz
132. Community involvement
133. Club and association memberships
134. Free directory listings
135. A tradeshow booth
136. Special events
137. A name tag at events
138. Luxury box at events
139. Gift certificates

140. Audio-visual aids
141. Flip charts
142. Reprints and blowups
143. Coupons
144. A free trial offer
145. Guarantees
146. Contests and sweepstakes
147. Baking or crafts ability
148. Lead buying
149. Follow-up
150. A tracking plan
151. Marketing-on-hold
152. Branded entertainment
153. Product placement
154. Being a radio talk show guest
155. Being a TV talk show guest
156. Subliminal marketing

Company Attributes

People are naturally attracted to companies that demonstrate specific attributes. The more of these attributes that you can claim for your company, the rosier our prediction of fame and fortune in your life. If your company comes up empty when assessing these attributes, remind your broker to sell short on your business. The truth is that the more of these attributes you have, the more poised you are for success. It's obvious right from the start. Company attributes are:

157. A proper view of marketing
158. Brand name awareness
159. Intelligent positioning
160. A name
161. A meme
162. A theme line
163. Writing ability

164. Copywriting ability
165. Headline copy talent
166. Location
167. Hours of operation
168. Days of operation
169. Credit cards acceptance
170. Financing availability
171. Credibility
172. Reputation
173. Efficiency
174. Quality
175. Service
176. Selection
177. Price
178. Upgrade opportunities
179. Referral program
180. Spying
181. Testimonials
182. Extra value
183. Adopting a noble cause

Company Attitudes

The company attributes we explored above were about your company. The company attitudes we list now are about your mind. All of these attitudes ought to be descriptive of your company, but in reality, they are descriptive of you. They begin with you. They flourish because of you. They win sales and profits because of you. Maybe 5,000 people help you do these things. But we know these attitudes come from your brain and rest on your shoulders. And we know how much they can mean to your company. The company attitudes are:

184. Easy to do business with
185. Honest interest in people
186. Good telephone demeanor

187. Passion and enthusiasm
188. Sensitivity
189. Patience
190. Flexiblity
191. Generosity
192. Self-confidence
193. Neatness
194. Aggressiveness
195. Competitiveness
196. High energy
197. Speed
198. Focus
199. Attention to details
200. Ability to take action

You've done a third of the job now. You've become aware of all 200 weapons of guerrilla marketing. Although it didn't take you long, that's a tremendous part of achieving victory and profits with guerrilla marketing.

We know we don't have to remind you of the second third of your job because you're so motivated to succeed, but still, we would be lax if we didn't. Experimenting with the weapons that feel right to you is going to take a lot longer than the first third, but it's a whale of a lot more fun. It's actually going out on a limb and investing your hard-earned time, energy, imagination, information, and perhaps your money in marketing. Then you've got to *pay close attention*. Some of your investments are going to fall flat on your hopes and dreams. Others are going to give you a happy surprise. You've just got to know which investments are souring and which are soaring. All marketing investments are not created equal. Some do sour, while others do soar. Are you going to know the difference? Are you going to be paying close enough attention?

The third third of your job is a happy one. It's giving the old heave-ho to those weapons that didn't earn their keep, didn't thrill you with their performance, didn't generate profits to warm you up from the inside out. Toss those investments in the junkyard. They have no place in any guerrilla's arsenal.

13

CREATING A SEVEN-SENTENCE GUERRILLA MARKETING PLAN

Of the important lists we set out for you, this next one is the easiest to remember and hardest to do. It's a list with only two items. The first item can be handled in five minutes. But the second item takes the lifetime of a business, which is one reason why it is so hard to do that it is commonly abandoned. Here's the list:

1. Start with a plan.
2. Commit to that plan.

That's the basic idea. That's the thing for you to know. Now that you know it, this is just the right time to go over the plan with you. It's your plan, your business, your future. So we're going to devote more time to talking about the plan than we will creating the plan. The result will be a private gold mine that can be yours after the plan is created.

This gold mine has seven sentences covering the most pressing issues in marketing. We know that there are far more than seven issues facing a company about to market. But we also know the close correlation between focus and profits. By all means, scrutinize every aspect of your business—you know the guerrilla's penchant for detail—but concentrate on these seven areas of marketing.

You'll prove your concentration with one brief sentence covering each area. That's not overly demanding. In fact, all the sentences except the fourth one are short and simple. The fourth one is a list.

A minute is a long time. Just stop doing everything for one minute and you'll see how much time is packed into that little unit. *If your start and your future with guerrilla marketing are going to succeed, you have to put into writing a seven-sentence guerrilla marketing plan. You'll have five minutes to do it. You know how long that is.*

If you're in this for the money, you'll write the plan at the best time—which is the moment you finish this chapter. But don't begin to write until you know what each of the sentences is supposed to cover. Don't try to cover too much or say too much in each of your sentences. A guerrilla marketing plan is a blueprint, a framework, a map with directions.

In addition to providing you with the right answers, furnished by you, the plan provides you with the right questions, furnished by us. If these right questions are combined with these right answers, you have something worthy of your commitment. If you move up the final step—the 200th guerrilla marketing weapon—and take action, you'll be joining the ranks of guerrilla marketers, marketing shepherds who have followed the precepts of guerrilla marketing to abundant money for themselves, their families, their businesses, their employees, their investors, and their charities.

What you're about to create will serve you in your start-up phase with guerrilla marketing and continue serving you for three to five years. Although your commitment to that plan is going to make it work, you must still be prepared to make minor alterations in the

> A guerrilla marketing plan is a blueprint, a framework, a map with directions.

plan, though we hope not. We hope you got it right the first time around.

A marketing plan that brief and focused has been the cornerstone for many businesses worldwide. It's short enough to show to all interested parties without boring them with details. It's focused enough so that everyone gets the point. Procter & Gamble, one of the world's most marketing-minded companies, creates a marketing plan for each of its products. Those plans are as brief as we're suggesting here. The P&G plan may be accompanied by 300 pages of documentation, but it begins with a clear guerrilla marketing strategy. You can and should do as you like with your own documentation. But first, get the seven sentences right. Write them with all seven as a single paragraph.

> *"Begin with the end in mind."*
> —STEPHEN COVEY

The First Sentence Tells the Purpose of Your Marketing

Be very specific, What physical action do you want your prospect to take? Pick up a phone and punch in your number? Click to your web site? Send an e-mail to you? Go to your store? Look for your product next time she's at a store? Call a phone number and ask for Cali Rose? What specific thing do you want prospects to do right after they've been exposed to your marketing message? You've got to be clear about that or your prospects never will be.

Don't say something obvious like "to grow," "to earn profits," or "to surpass my competitors." Instead, be very specific.

What exactly is the outcome you really want from your marketing? Begin by creating SMART goals: Sensible, Measurable, Achievable,

Be very specific, What physical action do you want your prospect to take?

Realistic, and Time bound (must be accomplished before a specified deadline). For example, maybe you want to develop 50 new leads by June 3rd, generate 1,000 web hits a day, cultivate ten new clients in the next three months, send 100 newsletters targeted to the most influential people in your industry, or develop a new brochure by September 1st.

Recognizing the success or failure of all steps that follow will be based on the clarity of your initial goals and purpose.

List some SMART goals for your business:

_____

_____

_____

_____

_____

Don't talk marketing or advertising in this sentence. Talk plain shirtsleeve English. We'd write a couple of examples here for you, but starting up does not mean hitching a ride. Delegate lots of things, but don't delegate the purpose of your marketing. Simply close your eyes

SMART GOALS

S = Sensible

M = Measurable

A = Achievable

R = Realistic

T = Time bound

and visualize a prospect who has just read, heard, or viewed your message. The prospect is smiling. What's he going to do next? Watch him carefully, then convince the world to do just what he did.

The Second Sentence States the Competitive Advantage You'll Emphasize

How will you accomplish your first sentence goal? Why will your public take that physical action we were just talking about? You've got a lot of benefits that you offer to your public, but so do your competitors. Fortunately for you, you've also got some benefits that only you offer. Those are your competitive advantages. That's where you hang your marketing hat. That's what you tell your marketing creative team to focus upon.

If you have multiple competitive advantages, good for you, but pick only one to be the superstar of your marketing. More than one might confuse an audience already besieged by marketing clutter.

If you can, stress the competitive advantage you offer so that it is seen as the solution to a problem. Guerrillas have long known that it's much easier to sell the solution to a problem than to sell a positive benefit. By including your competitive advantage in your marketing strategy, you won't be tempted to wander off down marketing side roads or neglect to mention the advantage in the first place.

> Your competitive advantages: That's where you hang your marketing hat.

> It's much easier to sell the solution to a problem than to sell a positive benefit.

The Third Sentence Tells Your Target Audience

The more specific you can be and the more you can narrow down the numbers, the more accurate you can be with your marketing's aim. Remember the new word you should know is "nanocasting." Your marketing plan should be as precise and focused as a nanocast.

Try to broadcast only to people with a very high propensity to want and need what you are selling. It is not a matter of big numbers as much as unswerving accuracy. Know that 1,000 of the big numbers

> Your marketing plan should be as precise and focused as a nanocast.

won't earn as much profit for you as ten of the right numbers. The equation to commit to memory is that in a successful marketing program, 10 percent of the credit goes to the creative work, 10 percent to the offer itself, 10 percent to the price, and 70 percent to the target audience.

It may be that you have more than one target audience. Many companies have several. If you're starting up a guerrilla marketing campaign right now, don't wait another moment before training your sights on your other target markets. If you don't, someone else probably will, and you'll have a devil of a time getting them back, if you get them at all.

FOCUSING ON YOUR CUSTOMER

A large copying company realized that as an industry, the legal sector churned out the most copies. It redirected some of its marketing budget, investing no extra money but simply aiming with more precision, and increased its profits 31 percent in one year. That's a whale of a lot of money for merely identifying a target market.

The Fourth Sentence Lists the Marketing Weapons You'll Be Using

Just flip back a few pages and you'll be supplied with 200 good ideas for using weaponry in your quest for profits. Until you've had real battlefield experience with these weapons, you'll have to go with your instinct, selecting weapons

1. that you can afford,
2. that you can understand, and
3. that you can use properly.

Only fools and nonguerrillas use weapons that don't meet those three criteria. It's much easier to abuse marketing weapons than to use them, so don't take any silly chances. One of the joys of guerrilla marketing is its encouragement to experiment. Make many of the little, inexpensive mistakes to avoid making any of the big, expensive ones.

Because you're aware of so many options, it ought to be easy for you to end up with an arsenal of custom-chosen weapons that have demonstrated their firepower in real battles. Far more weapons are affordable now than at any time in history. This is not your father's century. This is your century, and by properly equipping yourself for the struggle to win minds and money, you'll be in for a smooth and lovely ride.

The Fifth Sentence Tells Your Niche in the Marketplace

Now that you have determined your purpose, benefits, and target market, it's time to define your marketing niche. When people hear the name of your company, what's the first thing that enters their minds? Is it price, speed, economy, exclusivity, value, service, selection, or one of a host of other good things? That's your niche, also referred to as positioning, and it's what you stand for in the minds of your prospects. It is our hope that their take on you matches your own. If you want to be known for service, but you're mainly known for low prices, something's wrong.

> That's your niche, also referred to as positioning, and it's what you stand for in the minds of your prospects.

Guerrillas know that the marketplace is cluttered with competition and that it can really pay to be a leader in a smaller pond.

- Marty Winston is "the most e-mail knowledgeable PR agent in the universe."
- Sara Walker is the "ADD coach."
- Ingred Elsel is "an insurance agent specializing in mining companies."

Guerrillas carve out a position where they can differentiate them-selves and this differentiation is apparent in every marketing weapon they use. Niches can be defined in many ways, including through a specific target market or a distinct means of service. What's your niche?

Once you are clear about what your niche is, let it come shining through all of your other marketing. Act and live as though you're proud of it. Or else, move heaven and earth trying to change it. The best time to change it is never—because you got it right the first time and knew you had to wave it like a flag. Your target market has a hard time understanding why it should do business with you. Don't add confusion about you to the mix.

The Sixth Sentence Tells Your Identity

Your identity is different from your image, because an identity is based on truth while an image is based on fancy. "*Image*" is a word worth striking from your marketing vocabulary. An image defined in diction-aries as a façade, something phony. The far better "I" word is "*identity*." Your identity is automatically honest. If you communicate a real iden-tity, people sense feelings of comfort and relaxation when they contact you. What they see in your marketing is ultimately what they get from your goods and services, and that builds trust and rapport.

> An identity is partly your company personality.

An identity is partly your company personality. Every company has an identity. But many of those companies didn't give it much, if any, thought, so it's whatever the wind blows in and whatever the public has decided. If that's you, we've got a mission for you. Put your identity into writing, right in your marketing plan, so that it will apply to all creative materials you use for marketing. Tell the truth.

People are attracted to other people and businesses, who have pleasant or exciting personalities. Be great at your business. But don't be all business. Let your identity shine through.

Keep in mind that an image, "a façade," can get you in trouble. When people see that you're not quite who they expected you to be based on your marketing, they feel a sense of misrepresentation. That does not lead to bonding. If you say or act like you're something that you're really not, don't mention our name.

The Seventh Sentence States Your Marketing Budget, Expressed as a Percentage of Your Projected Gross Sales

The beauty of guerrilla marketing is that over half the marketing weapons are free. But, don't let that fool you; there are important reasons to spend money on your marketing.

Guerrilla marketers know that the most important place to spend money is on business presentations. This means the quality of your stationery, business cards, brochures, fliers, and logos. The public will get their first sense of your professionalism through your written materials, so make a strong impression. This may cost you some money, but look at it as an investment in your future.

Now spend a few minutes deciding where you'll get the biggest bang for your buck with your marketing dollars. Having a good idea of your budget helps you plan better and avoid many emergencies, not to mention avoid misspending precious marketing funds. Be sure to calculate your marketing budget using your projected gross sales because that helps you operate in a growth mode. If you work off your current sales, you'd be planning to tread water.

In 2007, the average U.S. business invested 4 percent of gross revenues in marketing. But the guerrilla knows what happens to the average U.S. business—it vaporizes within five years. So at the start, when you have the least money, you still ought to invest generously in your debut. You might invest 10 percent the first year, but rising sales would make that absolute dollar mount only 5 percent the next year and 3 percent after that. We know how you feel about this, but you have to pin down a number and write it into your plan as the seventh sentence.

> Be sure to calculate your marketing budget using your projected gross sales because that helps you operate in a growth mode.

Now you're ready to write a seven-sentence guerrilla marketing plan. There is no earthly reason why you should need more than five minutes to do it. We've been spending this whole chapter prepping you for the task.

> *Going into business without a guerrilla marketing plan is a lot like going to battle under a general who tells you: "Ready–Fire–Aim!"*

You've got to take an important step when you write your plan. Figure 13.1 is there to help you pull it all together. If you can't take this step, frankly, you ought to come back to this page when you are ready. The step is encapsulated in two brave words: *trust yourself*. Don't let uncertainty stop you. That first sentence ought to flow from your mind to your marketing and the next six sentences should go with that flow. All along, your unconscious mind knows the right things to say in your plan. These five minutes are when it reveals its brilliance to you.

FIGURE 13.1: **The Seven-Sentence Marketing Plan Worksheet**

1. The first tells the purpose of your marketing. _____

    _____

2. The second tells how to achieve the purpose, stressing benefits. _____

    _____

3. The third tells target audience or audiences. _____

    _____

4. The fourth tells marketing weapons you'll use. _____

    _____

5. The fifth tells your niche in the marketplace. _____

    _____

6. The sixth tells your identity. _____

    _____

7. The seventh tells your marketing budget as a percentage of your projected gross sales. __

    _____

Take five minutes now to put your marketing plan into writing, knowing it should guide you for the next three years, at the least. _____

_____

PLANNING A GUERRILLA MARKETING CALENDAR

It takes a year to create a solid guerrilla marketing calendar. It takes two years to create one that's outstanding. It takes three years to create a perfect one. Clients of ours who have one say that it's like getting into heaven without the inconvenience of dying.

A guerrilla marketing calendar provides you with several advantages: it's simple to prepare, it's free, it helps prevent marketing emergencies, it helps avoid missed deadlines, it aids in financial planning, it aids in hiring, and it automatically gets stronger each year.

We've seen that an hour is ample to create a one-year guerrilla marketing calendar. That means you spend one hour guiding your marketing efforts for one year. Your guerrilla marketing plan is your long-term road map to success. Your guerrilla marketing calendar is your short-term road map. They complement each other.

STRATEGY VERSUS TACTIC

In business, it's crucial to know the difference between strategy and tactics. Many business owners, confused about the difference, wander around and end up lost. Strategy is the guiding light that illuminates the path. The guerrilla marketing plan is a strategy. Tactics are the specific steps you take along that path, the copy, the price, the offer. The guerrilla marketing calendar is a tactic.

You need the plan in order to create the calendar. The plan will list the right target audience. The calendar will list the right weapons. The calendar has only 12 rows, one for each month of the year, and 5 columns (see Figure 14.1).

1. *The first column is Month* because it lists the months of the year. That's the easiest of the five columns.
2. *The second column is Message* because it states the thrust of your marketing that month. Were you having a sale? Did you feature new items? Were you having an event such as a show or a series of seminars? What was your marketing message?
3. *The third column is Media* because that's where you'll list the marketing weapons you'll be using that month.
4. *The fourth column is Money* where you put a dollar sign, because that's how you'll know exactly how much you invested in marketing that month.
5. *The fifth column is Grade*, and it's where you have the most fun, or the most agony. It's where you are transformed into a college professor and give the month a letter grade—an A, B, C, D, or F—to indicate how well (or poorly) your marketing served you that month.

It's true that at the end of one month, you can't definitively quantify your profits. But you can try. And you can be sensitive to your

Your guerrilla marketing plan is your long-term road map to success. Your guerrilla marketing calendar is your short-term road map. They complement each other.

"stomach reaction" to the month. Deep inside of you, you probably know that the month was a major moneymaker—or that it sucked in spite of your hopes, dreams, and financial investment. Put it in writing. Learn from it. Surpass it next time.

At the end of the year, a year from when you first planned your calendar, look carefully at each month's grades with your brutally honest gaze. Stop doing the things you did during months that received C's, D's, and F's. Don't have thrusts such as you had during those loser months. Avoid the media where you wasted your month's financial investment. Leave yourself with a calendar of only A's and B's.

But that's not good enough. During the planning of your next calendar, double up on the thrusts that worked on the last calendar. At the end of that next year, get rid of those thrusts that only merited a B. For the third year, each month should have the planning, thrusts, media, and the costs that were the stars of your A months. Each month should be planned to earn an A for you. Once you've got a calendar like that, hide it. Don't let your competitors have even a glimmer of an idea of why things are going so swimmingly for you and why you're always attempting to hide that smile on your face.

One of the best days of the year for you will always be that day when you look over your guerrilla marketing calendar and learn from it. That will be the day when you get to flex your strengths, eliminate your weaknesses, and realize that you've got a horse to ride next year, the year after that, and for a long as you're a guerrilla.

Sure, your calendar will change from year to year because marketing changes and new weapons become available. Competitors of yours will grow smarter and stronger themselves, or they'll disappear.

The same is true for your business. You're going to have a proven and a profitable marketing calendar. You're going to be tempted to repeat it the next year. Do just that. The year after, too. That's exactly what a savvy guerrilla should do. But be ready for change. Be ready to get smarter and stronger. Don't plan to make wholesale changes

> A year from when you first planned your calendar, look carefully at each month's grades. Stop doing the things you did during months that received C's, D's, and F's. Leave yourself with a calendar of only A's and B's.

and readjust your whole life. Instead, think tweak. Tweak your calendar to make it more precise, more deadly. The idea is to make few changes and only necessary ones. Make tweaking an annual habit.

FIGURE 14.1: **Sample Guerrilla Marketing Calendar**

Month	Message	Media	Money	Grade
January				
February				
March				
April				
May				
June				
July				
August				
September				
October				
November				
December				

ESTABLISHING A WEB SITE

The internet has revolutionized business. For the first time, owners of all sizes and types of businesses can communicate with prospects and customers at virtually no cost. These communications can be as colorful, detailed, and photo-filled as desired, without increasing per-message delivery costs.

At the same time, the internet has also spawned much hype and for many, disappointing results. Numerous business owners have been burned by so-called internet experts who may know the latest software programming tricks, but have had only limited marketing or sales experience. Guerrilla marketers know better than to trust the future of their businesses to outsiders who are not as familiar with their businesses as they are. As we have frequently found, knowledge permits planned action.

The purpose of this chapter is to review the basics of web marketing so you can take better control of your own web site, regardless of whether you design and maintain it yourself, or hire others to do so.

The Similarities of Web Marketing and Print Marketing

In many ways, the internet is more than just another marketing medium; it's a new medium requiring a different mindset. In other ways, the web resembles traditional print and broadcast marketing.

This is the first part of a two-part comparison. Here, we look at some of the ways web marketing resembles traditional print marketing and design such as brochures, newspaper advertisements, and newsletters. We analyze how web marketing builds on marketing and design techniques you're already familiar with. In the second part, we'll examine how web marketing and design differs from print marketing and design.

Planning

Both internet and print advertising succeed to the extent that they are goal-directed, focused on audience and message. Before you can begin working, you need a clear idea of the needs and attitudes of your audience and the action you want them to take. This means planning before action. You need to be certain of the purpose of your communication and the obstacles you must overcome to achieve it.

Theme

Both internet and print advertising succeed to the extent they are organized around a single central theme. Like symphonies, the most satisfying brochures, newsletters, and web sites are unified by a recurring theme, supporting the action you want your reader or web site visitor to take. The theme should appear on the front cover of your brochure, newsletter, or the home page of your web site, and

> Both internet and print advertising succeed to the extent that they are goal-directed, focused on audience and message.

should be repeated on each of the pages that follow. Each page of your brochure, newsletter, or web site should contain the central idea you're communicating.

Branding

Successful web sites, like effective ads, brochures, and newsletters, create a distinct visual format in the viewer's mind. Like an individual with a strong personality, successful marketing materials are memorable and stand out from the competition. Successful branding is based on the appropriate and consistent use of color, layout, type, and visuals.

> Successful branding is based on the appropriate and consistent use of color, layout, type, and visuals.

First Impressions

Brochure and newsletter readers, like visitors to your web site, are impatient. You have just a few seconds to capture their attention or they're gone forever. As the headlines and visuals on the front cover of your brochures and newsletters should attract your readers into turning the page, your home page should provide reasons for visitors to immediately begin following increasingly detailed links. Visitors to your web site will make "stay or move-on" decisions within seconds. Newsletters rely on a front page table of contents; home pages rely on graphics and highlighted text, which visibly links the visitor to the information inside.

Color

Color plays a major role in both print and internet advertising. Color operates emotionally, creating a mood or atmosphere that flavors your message. Always strive for appropriateness. Consider how inappropriate it would be to use Halloween colors, like black and orange, on your Christmas card or Christmas colors like red and green for invitations to your Halloween party. Color plays a pragmatic role.

Color also determines how easy your message is to read, requiring you to pay careful attention to foreground, text, and background colors. If there is insufficient contrast, your message will be hard to read and readers will likely pass it by. For example, blue text on a black or dark gray background, or purple on red, can be almost impossible to see. Likewise, color can be used as an attention-getting device to emphasize important messages: A red headline on a white background, for example, can make a special sale or promotion really jump.

White Space

Both print and internet advertising benefit from white space, empty areas of the page or screen that provide contrast to the adjacent text and graphics. White space provides breathing room for your text and reduces line length, making the text appear easier to read. White space also adds visual contrast to your pages and provides a resting spot for your reader's eyes. Still, if you can fill that white space with profit-producing copy, do it.

Accessibility

Both internet and print advertising succeed to the extent they are accessible. Information must be easy to locate rather than hidden in columns that contain paragraph after paragraph of text. In both print and internet advertising, information is communicated best when it is broken into short, bite-sized chunks and is easy to read. The easiest way to enhance readability is to employ frequent reader cues like headlines, subheads, department heads, and their web counterparts— links or bookmarks that take you to other parts of a single document.

Simplicity

Readers are busy. Both internet and print marketing fare best when marketing messages are simple to read. Simplicity requires short paragraphs, short words, and ruthless editing. Replace long words with short ones and delete all that are unnecessary.

Self-Interest

Internet and print marketing both succeed when they appeal to a reader's self-interest. Content and design decisions must be made with the reader in mind. Ask yourself:

1. *What* are the reader's problems?
2. *How* can my product solve them?
3. *What* evidence can I provide to back up my claims?
4. *How* can I employ design tools like color, type, and layout to make my message easier to read?

Marketing communications succeed to the extent they are designed to satisfy the reader, not the association, firm, or individual sending the message.

Call to Action

Both internet and print advertising succeed when there is a clearly identified call to action and when it is easy for the reader to respond. Direct mail that succeeds contains a toll-free 800 telephone number and self-addressed/postage-paid envelopes. Brochures and newspaper advertisements succeed when they feature large addresses and maps showing how to reach the business. Likewise, internet marketing succeeds when mechanisms are provided for the reader to register, making themselves available for later messages, to order the product via e-mail, or to contact the advertiser to request further information.

Web Marketing versus Print Marketing
Making the Most of Their Differences

We looked at how web marketing resembles print marketing. Now, let's examine the other side of the coin. Although internet and print advertising share many similarities, their differences are just as important. Acknowledging these differences is crucial to improving your ability to make the most of both traditional and new media.

Timing Is Everything

The size of a photograph doesn't matter when a reader encounters it in an ad, brochure, or newsletter; larger is often better. But the size of graphics in web communications can spell the difference between "read" or "not read."

Graphics must be as small as possible and designed for the lowest possible denominator of modem and connection speed. Readers are impatient and will quickly lose interest if forced to spend too much time waiting for pages to download.

Idea

If your web message depends heavily on photographs or detailed graphics, you might consider including two versions of each: "thumbnails," or small versions that when clicked, load larger versions. This way, casual visitors will know the photographs are available without sacrificing loading speed, while large versions will be available for those who are willing to wait to view them.

Navigation and Structure Are Crucial

Web communications require you to pay more attention to how a customer explores your information than print communications. Readers must be able to quickly locate the information you want them to read. Although it is likely that many readers will at least skim through every page of a brochure or newsletter, at least exposing them to headlines or subheads of possible interest, you can't assume web visitors are going to encounter every page of your web site. This places an added challenge to your home page. Web visitors are likely to make "continue" or "not continue" decisions based solely on what they encounter on your home page.

Instead of emphasizing your most important article on the front page along with a small table of contents, as is typical with print newsletters, you'll want your home page to hint at the primary article but place more emphasis on "teasers" that link visitors to features inside. Once inside your web site, icons, and other cues should make it easy for readers to quickly explore various topics of interest and to easily return to the first page.

Telegraphic Messages

Web writing is more challenging than writing for print. Web messages must be shorter and more telegraphic—more like billboards than ads, brochures, and newsletters—in order to compensate for the fact that many people dislike extended on-screen reading. This preference translates into shorter sentences and shorter paragraphs. In addition, subheads should appear both as links at the start of long articles and within the articles, allowing readers to quickly go directly to topics of interest. Likewise, summaries at the start of long articles can attract readers. Bulleted and numbered lists are another way to break long messages into short chunks.

Layout

Although multicolumn layouts are the norm for print brochures and newsletters, multicolumn layouts are less successful in web sites. Readers may find it hard to concentrate on a single column on a screen containing two or more parallel columns. Multicolumn formats also require scrolling, discouraging readers who don't want to be forced to scroll from the bottom of one column to the top of the next.

Number of Pages

There is a direct relationship between the costs of printing brochures or newsletters and the number of pages printed. Each page increases printing and, often, mailing costs. This isn't true with web publications. This means that, with the exception of internet service providers who charge by the number of pages, you can be far more flexible in your use of pages. You have the luxury of pages containing just a few words, such as a sidebar, and you can include a mini table of contents that breaks up long topics into manageable bite-sized chunks or lead visitors to other topics.

Color

Color is expensive in print communications. Although two-color printing doesn't mean twice the price of one-color printing, additional colors can quickly increase printing costs. Four-color printing of photographs is especially expensive and usually requires more expensive paper. Color is free on the web. This offers you far more flexibility for adding color to text or graphics and expands your ability to include colored graphics, allowing you to orchestrate responses by guiding readers and establishing the mood and image of your site.

Structured versus Unstructured

Most print communications are read in a linear, front-to-back manner. This gives the author/designer control over the sequence with which topics are encountered. Web documents, however, are nonlinear. Each web visitor is likely to explore your web site in a different sequence, investigating topics in a different order depending on what attracts their interest. This places an added burden on you to create a satisfying whole-out-of-the-parts that may be encountered in different order. It also forces you to spend more time creating links that will attract visitors to as many pages as possible, before departing.

Dynamic versus Static

Change is impossible once the printing press is turned on. Information is permanent in a print document. Tough luck if you change your mind or are forced to reschedule an event or run out of specially priced merchandise. Web documents are dynamic. You can change your web site every day or even every hour to reflect your current inventory or recommendations. Restaurants, for example, can post daily luncheon specials or their weekend entertainment.

Web marketing offers more, but requires more than simply posting existing ads, brochures, and newsletters to your web site. Web sites have to be designed from the ground up for on-screen reading.

Use the worksheet in Figure 15.1 to guide you in creating and maintaining the best possible web site. Each of the eight areas is critically important to your site's success.

To analyze your web site better, consider these questions:

- What is the immediate, short-term goal of your web site? Be specific.

FIGURE 15.1: **Evaluating Your Web Site Worksheet**

Score your performance each area, from one to ten (1 = poor, 10 = excellent). Then, write down what you must do to increase your score in each area.

	Score
1. *Planning*. Do you know exactly what you want to accomplish with your web site? _____	
2. *Content*. What information will best attract visitors to your site and keep them coming back on a regular basis? _____	
3. *Design*. There's a "hang or click" moment when people first see your site. Do you understand how design influences their choice? _____	

FIGURE 15.1: **Evaluating Your Web Site Worksheet**

	Score
4. *Involvement*. How effectively do you use interactive tools, like return-on-investment calculators, to involve visitors instead of having them just read?	
5. *Production*. How efficiently do you use easy-to-use software to get your message online as quickly as possible?	
6. *Follow-up*. How much time typically elapses between the time visitors e-mail you to ask questions and the time you respond?	
7. *Promotion*. How visible is your web site to search engines? Is it linked to other sites? Do you promote your web site off-line in media, mailings, and wherever your name appears?	
8. *Maintenance*. Do you consistently change, update, freshen, and renew your web site?	

- What specific action do you want visitors to take? Be specific.
- What are your objectives for the long term? Be specific.
- Who do you want to visit your site?
- What solutions or benefits can you offer to these visitors?
- What data should your site provide to achieve your primary goal?
- What information can you provide to encourage them to act right now?
- What questions do you get asked the most on the telephone?
- What questions and comments do you hear most at trade shows?
- What data should your site provide to achieve your long-term objectives?
- Where does your target audience go for information?
- How often do you want visitors to return to your web site?
- What may be the reasons you don't sell as much as you'd like?
- Who is your most astute competition?
- Does your competition have a web site?
- What are some ways you can distinguish yourself from competitors?
- How important is price to your target audience?

Incentives and Visitor Registration

Successful guerrilla marketers recognize that web sites cannot succeed if they are "one night stands." Success is based on repeat visits. Accordingly, on their first visit, you need to obtain your visitor's e-mail address plus their permission to communicate with them in the future.

Your goal is to obtain their e-mail address so you can establish proactive, ongoing communications with customers and prospects, often based on a monthly or bimonthly newsletter sent via e-mail. Future e-mails can then be used to both maintain top-of-mind awareness and drive visitors back to your web site whenever you post updated content.

A Matter of Control

Unless you obtain the visitor's e-mail address on their first visit, it's up to your visitor whether or not they ever again visit your site. But, once you obtain their e-mail address plus permission to contact them in the future via e-mail, you're well on your way to building a successful relationship.

There are three keys to success in obtaining e-mail addresses:

1. *Incentive.* You must develop an incentive to encourage visitors to submit their e-mail addresses.
2. *Simplicity.* You must make it as easy as possible for visitors to register.
3. *Privacy.* You must provide and live up to a privacy statement assuring visitors that you will not sell, share, or otherwise distribute their e-mail addresses to anyone else.

Successful Incentives

The best way to encourage visitors to subscribe to your e-mail newsletter is provide a good description of the contents of the newsletter and offer a registration incentive like valuable information that they will receive immediately. Just saying "Sign up for my newsletter!" is not enough. There is no benefit to that statement. Instead, describe the type of information your newsletter will include and how frequently they will receive it.

Content

Tie this to a registration incentive that has high perceived value and can be distributed via e-mail, preferably as an Adobe Acrobat PDF (Portable Document Format) file. Acrobat files enhance the value of your message by maintaining the original formatting of your document and permitting you to use various typeface designs to project an appropriate, easily-read image.

Educational Content

The content of your incentive should be strictly educational. Let the value of your words sell your competence. In your incentive, provide valuable information that relates to the type of product or service that you provide. Use this incentive to communicate your empathy for your prospect's problems and—without bragging or boasting—show him that you know how to solve his problem. A useful starting point for creating an informational incentive is to use a numbered list approach: "Ten ways to increase word-of-mouth referrals," "Eight clues to your inner passions," "Twelve ways to get your point across in meetings."

Delivery

The easiest way to deliver incentives is as e-mail attachments that are automatically sent to your visitors upon receipt of their e-mail address.

Simplicity

Make it as easy as possible for visitors to register to receive your incentive. Request the minimum amount of information. Provide two text boxes, one for visitors to insert their first name, one for their e-mail addresses. Obtaining your visitor's first name permits you to personalize your communications. Avoid asking for more information. You'll find that there is often an inverse relationship between the amount of information you ask for and the number of visitors who register.

Avoid Future Spam

Don't assume that everyone who wants your registration incentive also wants your e-mail newsletter. It's important for you to permit visitors to receive your registration incentive without having to subscribe to your newsletter. Accordingly, provide a special check box for visitors who want to receive your newsletter. This enhances your credibility and projects a professional image.

In addition, in each of the newsletters you send, remind subscribers that they have requested the newsletter. This reduces the possibility of complaints about your newsletter being unsolicited "spam."

The more opportunities you provide for visitors to sign up, the greater your response will be. Don't assume that a single registration form on the home page is enough. Success comes from the number of times visitors encounter your registration form. Many successful guerrillas provide a sign-up form at the bottom of every page.

Privacy

Place your privacy statement in a prominent location. State your intention to respect your visitors' privacy by never selling, sharing, or making their name and e-mail addresses available to anyone.

Registering Incentives
The Most Important Part of Your Web Site

The most important part of your web site is neither the home page nor any other individual page. Instead, the most important part of your web site is the *registration incentive* you offer to encourage visitors to submit their e-mail address to you. Your registration incentive determines the success or failure of your web site. Unless you succeed in obtaining visitors' e-mail addresses and permission to communicate with them, you may never get another chance to communicate. Once visitors leave your site, they're typically gone forever.

It costs you nothing to obtain permission to communicate with web site visitors and past customers via e-mail. Once you have this permission, you can establish a *trust-based relationship* that can reward you with years of profitable, repeat sales and word-of-mouth referrals. Choose an incentive you can deliver via e-mail because e-mail has great advantages for the guerrilla marketer:

- *Economy.* When you receive a request for information, you don't know the visitor's buying potential. It's imperative that you *not spend money* on visitors until you know their value.
- *Speed.* Delivery time is another reason to avoid conventional mail. Electronic incentives are delivered immediately, while snail mail may take days to arrive. By then, your web site visitors may have forgotten why they requested the incentive or—worse—fail to associate it with your web site.
- *Foreign.* Requests from abroad are another reason to offer electronic incentives. International postage costs more than domestic mail and usually takes more time to deliver.

Types of Incentives

Choose the form of incentive that your market will find most useful. Popular options include:

- *Buying information.* Many purchase decisions are made on the basis of price simply because buyers don't know how to shop for quality and value. You can gain an important advantage by showing your market how to be an intelligent buyer.
- *Glossaries.* Every field has its own specialized terms. Newcomers as well as experienced buyers appreciate better understanding the terms in your field.
- *Case studies.* Incentives showing how you successfully solved your client's problems permit you to use an editorial, as opposed to an advertising, tone. Case studies permit you to detail the benefits you helped clients overcome and the benefits they enjoyed.
- *Trends.* New technologies, challenges, and opportunities are constantly appearing. You very likely know more about changes in your field than your customers. Use this knowledge

to enhance your credibility by describing and interpreting the changes taking place.

Incentives don't have to be written. Your incentives might include spreadsheet templates that can be used to compute the benefits of buying from you or downloadable audiofiles of interviews or seminars. Screen savers permit visitors to view your craftsmanship on their monitors when they're not typing. *Let your imagination*—and understanding of your market's information needs—be your guide. Respect and trust are among the few things that money can't buy. Your competition may be capable of buying the market through extensive advertising or discounting, but *you* can *market information* that will help customers make *better buying decisions* and *enjoy full value* for years after they buy.

Incentive Marketing in Tough Times

The tighter money gets, the more carefully businesses and consumers spend their money and the more emphasis they place on trust and value rather than simply a low price. When times are bad, businesses and consumers don't stop buying. *They just spend their money more carefully.* You can also promote your incentives on the radio or in small ads to drive traffic to your web site. Use phone calls and postcards to encourage inactive past customers to register on your web site. Or use incentives to encourage readers of the print version of your newsletter to switch to the more economical e-mail version.

Alleviating Web Page Design Frustrations

Information is the ultimate reason for your web site's existence. Your web site should transparently communicate its content. Anything that interferes with the immediate and intuitive transfer of information between you and your web site visitor undermines your web site's success.

All too often, design interferes with communication. The following are our top eight web site design frustrations and suggestions showing how you can alleviate them. Use these as a guide to improving your own site.

1. *Long lines of text.* Long lines of text create boring, hard-to-read web sites. Visual boredom results when type extends in an unbroken line from the left to the right margin of the screen. Long lines are tiring because your eyes have to make long left-to-right shifts. It's also easy to get lost making the transition from the last word of one line to the first word of the next. Short lines of type create white space to the left and right of each line of text, framing your message. They also provide space to place secondary text or visual information.

2. *Large, meaningless graphics.* Large graphics take longer to download than small graphics. Long downloading times are justified if the result is meaningful information. All too often, however, your reward for waiting for a graphic to download is only a large logo or an overly complicated image map. Respect your web site visitors' time. Restrict large graphics to occasions where they communicate valuable information. Equally important when including photographs, use thumbnails—or reduced size images—that visitors can click on to load larger versions.

3. *Bright backgrounds.* Bright colors have their place on the web, but usually not as background colors. Large amounts of bright reds, oranges, yellows, or lime green backgrounds are visually tiring and certain to reduce the time visitors spend at your site. Instead, choose subdued background colors. Restrict bright colors to a few high-impact words, illustrations, or graphic accents.

4. *Dead ends and broken promises.* Strive for consistency. Anything that looks different is likely to be interpreted as a link. Many web sites, for example, use subheads set in a different color than the text they introduce. These can be easily confused with

links. Always check and double-check links to make sure they lead to the information they promise. Avoid links to pages that do not contain the promised information. Avoid links to "work-in-progress" locations.

5. *Lack of consistency*. Consistent colors, layouts, and type enhance your firm's image and project credibility and professionalism. Your firm's image is undermined when different colors and layouts are used on different pages of your site. You'll frequently encounter well-designed home pages where the text is neatly indented from the edges of the screen, but when you get deeper into the site, you encounter different background colors and long lines of text. Change undermines credibility and can cause visitors to wonder if they've visiting a different site.

6. *Pages that cannot be printed*. Whenever we encounter a web page we might want to refer back to later, we print it out. This works well, unless the text was set in a light color like white or yellow against a black or blue background. When you print from your browser, the web page's background color is not printed. This means you print white or yellow ink on white paper—hardly readable! If there is any chance at all your web site visitors may want to print your pages, avoid light text colors.

7. *Unnecessary graphic accents*. Graphic accents, like horizontal rules dividing topics, can easily clutter-up a page and project an amateurish "My First Web Site!" image. Instead of using horizontal rules to break up a long articles, insert subheads that preview the text that follows. To reinforce the impact of the subheads, set them bold and surround them with white space above and below them.

8. *Oversize pages*. Many web sites force visitors to scroll sideways, in order to see the endings of words along the right-hand margin. This is unsightly and frustrating. It is often caused by long words placed in table columns too narrow to accommodate them. When using tables to organize text placement, check

every page before posting it. Build in a margin for error by searching for short words to replace long words.

Be More Observant

Training yourself to become a critical observer of other web sites is the first step towards improving your own web site. Get in the habit of carefully analyzing the sites you visit, especially those of your competitors. Then, see how your own site stacks up. Below are some things to look for as you evaluate the web sites you visit:

- *Speed*. A fast-loading home page speed is critical to the success of any web site. If visitors have to wait for large graphics to download, they are likely to leave and visit another site.

- *Site purpose*. The firm or organization's products, services, or goals should be immediately obvious. What type of activities does the firm or organization engage in? Who do they serve?

- *Engagement*. You should be able to immediately understand the benefits or information the firm or organization offers you. Prospective clients or supporters should be able to immediately see how a relationship with the web site offers both short-term and long-term benefits

- *Navigation*. How easy is it to locate desired information? Your ability to locate information, regardless of whether it refers to editorial content, product information, shipping costs, or e-mail address, is of paramount importance. Information is useless if it cannot be quickly and easily located.

- *Usability*. Usability refers to ease of reading and chunking. Ease of reading is based on relatively short lines of text and freedom from distractions, like bright-colored backgrounds or distracting textures. Chunking refers to breaking information into bite-sized units using short paragraphs introduced by frequent subheads. Bulleted or numbered lists also permit visitors to grasp an article's contents at a glance.

- *Timely*. How up-to-date is the information on the web site? Web site credibility plummets if the home page promotes an event that occurred two months ago. Web sites should be considered works in progress that are constantly updated, if only so that they don't bore repeat visitors.
- *Design*. Is the design appropriate for the firm or organization it serves? Layout, colors, and typefaces determine the site's personality and image.
- *Technology*. Is technology used appropriately to increase the site's information value or is technology used decoratively, in a show-off fashion? Sound, video clips, and animation can either enhance or hinder communication.
- *Call to action*. Does the site encourage you to take the next step, such as request more information or make a purchase?

Get in the habit of critically evaluating at least one or two web sites every day and taking careful note of your impressions. You'll be surprised at the many lessons you learn that can apply to your web site. Soon, the habit of critical evaluation will be second nature to you.

Your web site must be visible in order to draw traffic, and 84.8 percent of web site traffic comes from search engines. Good search engine placement is crucial for visibility.

Your marketing efforts will only be successful if customers view you as credible. Take the time to distribute useful information to your prospects. This will demonstrate your expertise and professionalism. The number-one factor in influencing purchase decisions is confidence. And the road to confidence is paved with credibility. Having the lowest price, widest selection, or most convenience won't help you much if your prospect doesn't trust you in the first place.

Some ways to inspire credibility:

- Be consistent in your marketing message.
- Use testimonials liberally.
- Have professional marketing materials.
- Try for frequent visibility.

- Focus on what your customer wants and needs.
- Give prompt responses to inquiries.
- Pay attention to details.
- Be generous with information.
- Make the purchase as easy as possible.
- Be accessible to your prospect.
- Offer excellent customer service.
- Strive for a good reputation.
- Be incredibly honest.
- Take responsibility.
- Treat people fairly.
- Offer an unconditional guarantee.
- Give free samples of your products.
- Be an expert.
- Talk to your customers.

BUILDING AN EFFECTIVE WEB SITE

Does your web site:

- Load quickly?
- Communicate your area of expertise?
- Describe the products or services offered?
- Offer information that will benefit visitors?
- Describe your unique competitive advantage?
- Invite visitor participation?
- Create a sense of professionalism?
- Establish credibility?
- Include contact information on every page?
- State the length and terms of your guarantee or warranty?

- Give a little more than is expected?
- Resolve disputes in favor of your customer, whenever possible?

The internet can be an incredibly lonely place. Working to establish relationships can overcome the web's namelessness and help build trust with your prospects. Customers can't see the smile on your face when they type in your URL. They can't hear your reassuring hello as they walk through your cyberdoor. Yet, the online relationship-building process must begin immediately. Visitors will decide in seconds whether to stick around or click away. They tend to be an impatient lot and will be quickly agitated if you don't tell them right away what they can expect from your site.

Effective web sites are not based as much on mastering the internet and software technology as they are on applying tried-and-proven guerrilla marketing techniques to your web site. The most beautiful, technically sophisticated web site in the world will fail if it is not built around providing meaningful content that visitors want or on motivating visitors to take the action that the firm wants.

Once you have established goals for your web site, it is relatively easy to master the appropriate software needed to accomplish it or

WEB SUCCESSES

Once again, success comes down to answering basic questions:

- Who is your market?
- What information do people need in order to want to take the action you desire?
- What are you doing to make sure your target market visits, and revisits your web site?
- Does your web site provide a pleasant visiting experience?

hire the right people who already know how to do what needs to be done.

Automating Your Web Site

The amazing growth of the internet has created new-found opportunities for millions of businesses that previously would have never been able to compete in the global marketplace. Yet while the low entry and marketing costs have leveled the playing field for many entrepreneurs, they have also created a staggering amount of competition.

The average person, at least those who live in metropolitan areas, is exposed to more than 3,700 old media and new media marketing messages a day. To make online sales even more difficult, marketing studies have shown that it takes nine or more impressions for your business to be patronized by a new customer. This means follow-up is essential. Many online businesses accomplish it with online marketing automation.

Imagine being able to capture new leads on your web site, build customer confidence through automated sequential responses, deliver products digitally while you sleep, and track all of your prospects and clients without lifting a finger. For thousands of online businesses, this happens every day. In today's competitive environment, automation is not a luxury; it's a requirement for keeping the competitive edge you need. In fact, the benefits of automation are so numerous you can't afford to ignore them.

We see five steps to online success:

1. *Capture e-mail addresses*. Your list is your gold mine. It is critical to all your marketing and is literally your most valuable asset. To build your mailing list, it is essential that you make a compelling offer. "Sign up for my mailing list" is no longer enough. Try something like this: "Free Special Report: The Five Keys to Dramatically Boosting Your Web Site Traffic in 30 Days."

Through online automation, you can offer digitally down-loaded special reports, e-newsletters, mini-educational courses, or free trials to entice visitors to share their name and e-mail address. When their data is entered, it is automatically placed in your database and can be programmed to trigger autore-sponders, which are one or multiple automated messages. Share your privacy policy below your opt-in box and give assurances that people can unsubscribe at any time. And of course, never spam anyone.

2. *Set up sequential autoresponders.* A very effective way to build trust with your prospects is to offer a mini-course that delivers content-rich, relevant information to your opt-in subscribers. These automatically distributed e-mail messages not only pro-vide content, but also motivate prospects to revisit your site for the latest offers. And of course, once they click through to your web site, you can offer more content delivered via audio, video, and other multimedia options as well as offers for your prod-ucts and services. Because studies shows that 48 percent of salespeople give up after the first contact and 25 percent after the second, this is a perfect way to make sure your follow-up stays consistent. Best of all, after you program the series, it will perform flawlessly for you for years to come.

3. *Take payments online.* It has never been easier or more affordable to set up online payment systems through PayPal or your own merchant account. And once you set up your payment account, it is very easy to sell products or services online by purchasing an online shopping cart. A shopping cart will allow you to cap-ture e-mail addresses, automate responses, track leads, and then sell your product to customers around the world 24/7. These systems are surprisingly easy to set up, operate, and maintain.

4. *Track and measure your marketing.* Here you must consider a number of questions when tracking your marketing:
   • How many unique visitors come to your web site?

- How many visitors opt-in to your mailing list or order your products?
- When you send e-mails, how many are opened and how many people actually click through to your web site?

The reason these metrics are so important is because if you don't know these stats, you won't know what to improve. It could be variables like the pulling power of your headlines, the copy, or navigation on your web site. You won't know until you start measuring. Many of today's automated systems include ad trackers that automatically calculate your click-throughs and conversion statistics.

5. *Free yourself up to work ON your business not just IN your business.* When you automate daily tasks you gain more time to focus on priorities for the strategic growth of your company. This new-found discretionary time comes without your money-making activities coming to a halt, or hiring and training staff. Also, when your business becomes automated, your presence becomes optional, leaving you time to take a vacation while still making money. With most systems you can quickly and easily check your sales and orders from any web browser.

The internet is a competitive, ever-changing marketplace. The right strategy combined with powerful and practical systems gives you an edge over your competitors. You'll attract more customers and spend less time, money, and energy winning them over. Automation services and software leverage the best technology available.

Effective E-Mail

Format your e-mail as carefully as your postal mail. Your presentations are not limited to print communications and your web site. You also present yourself every time you send e-mail to a client. Every e-mail you send is a point of customer contact. E-mail deserves as much attention as the most expensively printed brochure or newsletter. Every e-mail offers clients another opportunity to

Format your e-mail as carefully as your postal mail.

judge your competence and professionalism. Here are ten points you might want to review:

1. *Begin with a meaningful subject line.* Always identify the purpose of contents of your e-mail in the subject line. At best, an obscure or missing subject line may relegate your e-mail message to the "read when I get around to it" category. At worst, in this age of computer viruses, if visitors don't immediately recognize the sender's e-mail address and there is a missing or ambiguous subject line, your client might immediately delete your message.

2. *Avoid run-on replies.* A run-on reply occurs when you and your client send multiple responses to previously sent and received e-mail. After two or three replies to previous messages, each with the same subject line, it becomes difficult for both sender and recipient to remember the subject under discussion. Instead, break the chain and send fresh e-mail, perhaps one that begins with a summary of previous communications. Otherwise, it will be difficult for you or your client to know which is the latest and most important message.

3. *Always include a salutation.* Even if it's the fifth e-mail in a row that you've sent your client, don't jump into the text. Instead, insert a "Dear (name):" salutation. Your client will appreciate your politeness. Most of today's e-mail programs include a mail merge feature that make it easy to personalize your e-mails by inserting your client or prospect's name in the salutation. This technique goes a long way toward making your e-mails stand out.

4. *Keep lines short.* One of the best ways to project a professional image is to restrict line length to approximately 40 characters. Recipients of your e-mail will find short lines of text far easier to read than text that extends the full width of their e-mail browser. They will appreciate the pool of white space to the right of your message.

5. *Keep paragraphs short and well-spaced.* Limit the number of sentences in each paragraph even more than you might in print or on the web. Edit your message to the bone, and then press the "Enter" key twice at the end of each paragraph to force extra space between the paragraphs.

6. *Chunk your message.* If your e-mail addresses two or more topics, use subheads to identify different topics and add visual interest. Most programs permit you to apply bold formatting to subheads.

7. *Provide a table of contents.* If your e-mail covers several topics, copy and paste the subheads to the top of your e-mail, below the salutation, so recipients can see the topics covered in your e-mail the instant it opens, without scrolling.

8. *Use your spellchecker!* E-mail programs differ in their ability to spellcheck your message before it is sent. Some programs correct your spelling while you type, some wait until the end. Other programs check your entire message, others fail to spellcheck your subject line. Spelling errors are very noticeable in e-mail messages. Whenever possible, set your e-mail program up to automatically spellcheck your message before it is sent.

9. *Use HTML e-mail with restraint.* Although it is possible to add your logo and other graphics to your e-mail, this slows down the recipient's computer and often forces your prospect to increase the screen size. To maximize the effectiveness of your e-mail, restrict the use of formatted HTML e-mail to cases where you know clients will appreciate the added touch.

10. *End your e-mail at your signature.* Always insert a personal closing, "Best wishes," "Sincerely," or "Have a good weekend" to your e-mail, even if it's the fifth e-mail of the day. Avoid inserting anything important after your signature. Many people stop reading when they encounter your name, even if you have included an important p.s. E-mail is not just

an inexpensive way to communicate. It is not a second class citizen that doesn't have to be taken seriously. E-mail is as much a presentation tool as your newsletter, web site, telephone calls, and face-to-face client meetings.

Profiting from Your E-Mail List

Here are ways that you can take your new subscribers from just getting to know you to taking actions that make you money.

Step 1. Give them more value once they subscribe. Plan on at least seven to ten e-mails to your new subscriber that offer articles, cool resources, teleseminars on topics of interest, goodies they can download FREE. Then, you will have laid the groundwork for an important psychological response. People have a tremendous need to reciprocate when someone gives them something. So if you give your list lots of value and help them get what they want, you will find that when you ask them to take a look at a product or service that you offer, they will be predisposed to do what you ask.

Once you have established that bond with your new subscribers, you are in a position to make sales and in a much stronger position than all the other marketers out there who have simply been blasting out hype trying to get attention. Make sure that when you send your new subscriber e-mails, your reply address is always the same so they recognize that it's coming from you. You also want to make sure that you write subject lines in your e-mails that generate curiosity so your subscribers almost have to open them to find out what you've got in store for them.

Step 2: Review other people's products and make recommendations. A powerful way to make money online is to register as an affiliate of companies that sell products that offer true value to your subscribers. You can then tell your subscribers about these products. When they visit the special web sites that you send them to, you receive credit for any sales that result from your referral. Typically you will get anywhere from 10 to 50 percent commission on each sale you refer, depending on the program, and this can add up to serious money once you have enough subscribers.

With higher ticket items your commission could be $100 to $500 or more, so even a few sales can add up quickly. The advantage to offering reviews of other people's products and referring your subscribers is that you can further build goodwill by telling them about great products while not directly selling them anything of your own. This positioning reduces the natural resistance new subscribers have to being sold and allows you to make money while you build up the relationship. Make sure that you give honest reviews based on your personal experience with these products. Don't just send out marketing materials for any product if you want this strategy to work. Remember, you are building trust with your subscribers and your honest, objective opinion about products and services that you recommend is what they expect from you.

Step 3: Establish trust as an expert. Once your list trusts you as an expert, eventually they will want to buy a product from you. The very nature of the bonding process demands this, and you can see that when you have a list clamoring to buy products from you, there is hardly a better situation you could ask for. And, all you really need to do to produce products that your list will buy is to survey them and find out what they want or what they are having problems with. Then, you can either create a product that gives them what they asked for or you can hire someone do it for you to your specifications.

Step 4: Offer consulting and coaching with your subscribers. A natural progression from creating products is offering a limited amount of your time for consulting with and coaching your subscribers. You will get requests for one-on-one time with you, and if you position yourself correctly, you will be able to charge a high rate per hour and work only with the clients you choose. This can be a fantastic income stream and can lead to more product ideas as you get to know your subscribers better and find out what they want at a deeper level.

Step 5: Organize live events such as retreats and seminars. This is where you can bring together a large group of your subscribers to hear you and other speakers talk about subjects of interest. There is a huge opportunity to charge admission for these events as well as to sell more products and consulting from the speakers themselves.

16

FUSION
MARKETING

Yes, of course you can succeed on your own. No, you don't need anyone's help to achieve your goals. But if there are people who can help you, giving more than they ask, why would you disdain them? There can only be one answer: You don't understand how fusion marketing works and you don't know how to go about selecting the right partners.

When we say the word "partner," we don't mean it in the legal sense. We refer not to marriage, but to a fling. If it's fun, you'll do it again. If it's not, you learned a lesson. The whole concept of fusion marketing is based upon the "I'll scratch your back if you scratch mine" theory of social interaction.

You're doing favors for each other. The guiding lights are bright: Set up every fusion marketing arrangement so that there are three winners—you, your partners, and your customers. If just two of those three came out on top, you didn't set it up right.

Finding a Fusion Partner

Fusion marketing has been around for a long time. It used to be called "tie-ins with others," "collaborative marketing," or "co-marketing." But whatever the term, it always means that entrepreneurs have discovered the one of secrets of free enterprise and that they're flexing their newfound knowledge.

The gas station across from the video store says, "Mention my name and you'll get a free video from that store." The video store

> When we say the word "partner," we don't mean it in the legal sense. We refer not to marriage, but to a fling. If it's fun, you'll do it again.

MAKING CONNECTIONS

There's a large video store chain that's located only in shopping centers. It's a franchise, only it's different from other franchises. Rather than owning one franchise, which is the norm in the franchise biz, the average franchisee owns five franchises. One owns 22. How did this happen? Fusion marketing is the answer.

The franchisor said that as a condition of franchise, each franchisee had to establish 20 fusion marketing arrangements within a year. Most did it within a month. They'd walk into other businesses in the same shopping center saying: "We'll put a pack of brochures about your business at our cash register if you do the same for us." "We'll put your business card in our bags if you do the same for us." "We'll refer your business to our customers if you do the same for us." I'm sure you get the idea.

These guerrillas were able to spread the word about themselves and say it to more people, but it didn't cost them any money to power up their campaign this way because they were sharing the cost with others.

owner says, "Mention my name and you'll get one gallon of gas for free" (this is before gas was the price of lower than the cost of a new automobile). The concept is clear, and everyone seems to want to do it. It makes so much sense. It makes so much money.

Another way to do fusion marketing is by finding companies that have the same prospects as you, and then doing a favor for the owner of that business. A savvy restaurant owner knew the value of asking the guerrilla question, "What other businesses do my customers patronize?" Realizing that competition was fierce in her neighborhood, this owner used imagination rather than pure marketing dollars to spread the word of her fabulous food. She distributed coupons for two free dinners to all the hairstyling salons within a one-mile radius of the restaurant.

This was not a buy-one-get-one-free coupon, nor did it have limits, such as you had to eat on a Wednesday before 5 P.M. It was two free, no-strings-attached dinners, complete with wine and dessert. Of course the stylists checked out the restaurant. Because the food was as marvelous as advertised, the hairstylists talked it up to every one of their customers at the salon! As you know, gobs of information are exchanged at hairstyling salons and barbershops. News spread fast. Her business became the talk of the town. The restaurant owner had lines out the door, all because she was able to identify the hairstyling salons as the pulse of the community, and then did a favor for the owners.

If you think we're enthusiastic about fusion marketing, you ought to visit Japan where the business community has elevated it to art form. *Fortune* 500 companies fuse with mom-and-pop operations around the country in fusion and financial harmony. Companies become household words on a handshake and a smile. As many as 50 different companies are involved in many of those happy fusion partnerships. It's happening where the entrepreneurial spirit thrives.

For you to emulate the success of others who have beefed up their guerrilla marketing with the potency and economy of fusion marketing, remember the guerrilla mantra: "Do what works."

> Set up every fusion marketing arrangement so that there are three winners—you, your partners, and your customers. If just two of those three came out on top, you didn't set it up right.

Seek out fusion partners
- with the same kind of prospects as you.
- with the same high standards as you.
- who are willing to share the workload.
- who are upbeat people and not moaners.
- who have creative fusion marketing ideas themselves.

You probably won't find that fusion marketing partners are the making of your business, but you'll find many who are able to give your business a boost. Don't forget that partners help each other, so do what you can to make your fusion partner's business as profitable as possible.

Because you're a guerrilla in the start-up phase of your guerrilla marketing, you may have discovered a kindred spirit who can set the right example, walk the right path, and fusion market each other's offerings like there's no tomorrow. Select three potential fusion marketing partners and ask the following questions:

1. Why is this partnership appealing to me?
2. What assets do I bring to this partnership?
3. What products, programs, and services would I like to develop in this partnership?

LEADS CLUBS

In many world cities, lawyers, accountants, and insurance agents form "leads clubs," where they keep track of their new leads, especially the e-mail addresses. Each month, they meet and trade leads. These people have the same kind of prospects, the same lofty (cross your fingers here) standards, and the same positive attitude. With all that going for them, plus their willingness to try fusion marketing, they've got the making of guerrillas.

4. What resources will be needed to make this work?

Becoming a Resource

Becoming a resource increases your credibility and visibility to potential fusion marketing partners. Fusion marketing partners seek out those who earn their respect and already enjoy their market's respect. Here are some of the ways you can become a resource by providing meaningful and wanted information.

25 Ways to Become a Resource

1. Write articles for publication.
2. Teach a class.
3. Offer to help a friend in your area of expertise.
4. Do free consultations.
5. Publish an e-newsletter.
6. Print a newsletter.
7. Recommend your friend's, client's, and colleague's products and services whenever possible.
8. Market their products and services in combination with yours.
9. Involve them in a project you're doing.
10. Provide free community help.
11. Put information, surveys, tips, and articles on your web site.
12. Sponsor a charitable event.
13. Compile a list of recommended books in your area of expertise.
14. Link others' web sites on your web site.
15. Provide referrals.
16. Do a radio or TV spot.
17. Offer to be a free resource for prospects.
18. Send relevant articles to prospects and customers.
19. Donate time to a relevant association.
20. Work a trade show booth.

21. Connect people in all areas of your life.

22. Do a free seminar on a popular topic.

23. Send a yearly industry review to customers and colleagues.

24. Mentor someone.

25. Share information beyond your career expertise, such as travel knowledge, or hobbies.

What Do You Bring to a Fusion Partnership?

We started this chapter by helping you identify potential fusion marketing partners. An important part of this search involves taking stock of what you bring to the partnership. In particular, what are the qualities that fusion marketers look for in partners and how can you make yourself as attractive as possible to others? Use the worksheet in Figure 16.1 to help you identify those attributes and detractions.

As countless guerrilla marketers have seen, success in fusion partnering comes from the same tactics that make you valuable and attractive to potential buyers of your product and service. To the extent that you're a resource, one who is always ready with an answer or a suggestion, you become increasingly attractive to fusion marketing partners.

FIGURE 16.1: **Assess Your Partnership Potential**

Rate yourself as a fusion marketing partner. Review the following list and place a check next to the characteristics that describe you:

❑ I am opportunity oriented.

❑ I see multiple options.

❑ I have both a business and marketing plan.

❑ I am open to change.

FIGURE 16.1: **Assess Your Partnership Potential, continued**

- ❏ I value synergy.
- ❏ I place a high priority on customer service.
- ❏ I seek creative solutions to conflict.
- ❏ I see the "we" in winning.
- ❏ I have strong business relationships.
- ❏ I readily give and receive information and ideas.
- ❏ I demonstrate trustworthiness.
- ❏ I trust others.
- ❏ I use my intuition in decision making.

Rate yourself on qualities that make you less attractive to potential fusion marketing partners. What can you do to improve these problem areas?

- ❏ I am problem focused.
- ❏ I tend to see few options.
- ❏ My business and marketing plans are weak or absent.
- ❏ I am reluctant to shed old methods and approaches.
- ❏ I see only the "I" in winning.
- ❏ Customer service is not a top priority.
- ❏ I have limited or no other business relationships that support business growth.
- ❏ I rely exclusively on hard data for decision making.
- ❏ I am hesitant to give information and ideas.
- ❏ I value control.
- ❏ I don't easily trust others.
- ❏ I rarely demonstrate trustworthy behavior.

17

LAUNCHING YOUR ATTACK

When you first picked up this book, as much as you wanted to launch guerrilla marketing attack, you just weren't ready. Now, you're ready. Now, you have the equipment and know how to succeed with your attack. Never forget that anyone can launch an attack; only half of those will succeed. To be in the half that makes all the bank deposits, you've got to follow a ten-step process. Each step sets a foundation for the attack. As you've been reading these chapters, we've been revealing the intricacies of each step, and you've been learning them at the pace you need.

This is the chapter where you start doing. You've been learning during the past chapters, even doing during some of them. But the very foundation, the infrastructure of your guerrilla marketing attack is right here where you take that giant step from education to action. All of the steps except one are easy steps to take. Even a caveman could take them.

You must take them in order. Starting up means starting at the beginning, and for your attack, that's the first step. But this step is a lot different than those you've taken before. This is a nasty step. This one is gritty and definitely not for sissies.

This step, launching your guerrilla marketing attack, is one that should be taken in slow motion. You've never in a hurry to launch your attack. You're so ready and have planned so well, that there's no rush, no missed deadlines, no egg on anyone's face.

Here's how you launch in slow motion:

1. Put the weapons you're going to use *into priority order*. You may fire several weapons at once, but you surely won't pull the triggers on all of them at the same time. Relax. Take deep breaths.

2. When listing those weapons, put down the date they'll be launched. Don't rush, but don't dawdle, and whatever you do, tell the truth. Your grasp of reality is a make or break strength in this arena. Don't write a date that you want. Write a date that won't drive everyone crazy.

3. On that same list, next to each weapon, put the name of the person responsible for getting maximum firepower from it and include timing, targeting, technology, and tracking. For each weapon, there must be someone in charge. Ideally, that someone will be you—almost all the time. For those other times, be sure you put the name of a person who can handle the job as deftly as you or better.

4. Realize that you are the general and that a day will arrive that is the *first day listed on your launch plan*. That's the day to do your mailings, unveil your perfected web site, make those phone calls, get that PR story in the paper, and juice up the buzz with a party, maybe with a celebrity.

Launching your attack is D-Day to you. That's when the all the systems are in place and all the troops are ready to show how pleased they are that a prospect calls or happens by. There are no bullets flying. There are no shells soaring overhead. There are no planes in

> Launching your guerrilla marketing attack is one that should be taken in slow motion.

darkened skies. What there is is silence. Unless the phone rings or someone's got the TV on, that's the sound of a marketing attack. Oh, you can turn up the commercial on the radio or TV, but you can't really read the e-mail aloud or make telemarketing calls to each other.

The launching of a guerrilla marketing attack takes place on your part by planning and inaugurating new systems and campaigns, and by that faithful ally, your commitment. What takes place on the part of your prospects is nothing. They don't know that anything's different. Maybe they see you on the media or glance at an article about you in the newspaper, possibly even read a blurb about you online. But they've got a life to lead and they can't spend their time monitoring your marketing. Your competitors might and should notice, but most of your prospects are oblivious except for the ones you invited to your launch party where you aired one of your 30-second TV spots.

Here's where patience fits in—or else. You launch a well-planned campaign and nothing happens. Give it time. This is marketing, not war. When you launch an attack, there will be no casualties at first. There will be no visible signs of victory or defeat. The launching of an attack is an all-the-time thing; it's not a one-time thing. You have to pound away to make your point. You can't really let up, or it will appear as though you don't really take yourself seriously. A show of strength must be followed by real strength.

What you sense after launching the attack is a feeling of slow motion with consistent progress. Your attack is a river of lava, slowly flowing. You are not expecting miracles. You need to know that the attack you have launched will manifest itself in profits in a matter of weeks, or maybe months, or perhaps as long as a year, but manifest itself it will.

Those who expect too much of a marketing attack often become addicted to discounting, training the public to wait for sales. When they do not witness instant wealth, they cease their attack, leaving their public befuddled as to whether this company believes in itself or not. People want to do business with rock solid landmarks. And that

> Those who expect too much of a marketing attack often become addicted to discounting, training the public to wait for sales.

is exactly what you will become the day your launch your guerrilla marketing attack. You won't achieve your landmark status overnight. But if you aggressively—not expensively—market after your launch, you just might achieve landmark status and become a people magnet.

18

MAINTAINING YOUR CAMPAIGN

We've already warned you that the toughest part of your guerrilla marketing program will be maintaining it. Creating it and launching it are relative pieces of cake compared with the nerves of titanium you'll need to withstand the apathy and the competition standing in your way.

This chapter is not so much about the program as it is about you. Creating and launching the program were technical matters. Maintaining that program—sticking with it in spite of a zero percent return on your investment—is all about you, the inside core of you in the face of withering inattention and blistering rejection.

If you didn't know that inattention and rejection were part of the whole start-up phase of a marketing program, you'd pretty much sink at the start. At least we're warning you. You will not be surprised. That readiness, that acceptance of the early-going fate of the start-up business, that realization that hardly anything you want will come to you as soon as you want it—those critical factors will be amongst your best defenses against the start-up blues.

You know it's going to take several months for things to start falling in place for you, for you to make some timely adjustments in your original plan. You already expect that the marketing will not be paying its own way while it's still a baby, so you're in this all by yourself. It's your word, and ours, against a powerful wave of indifference by your market. But you're going to win this one . . . and we suspect you already know why.

You'll win it because you know the awesome power of commitment and the way it transforms indifferent people into loyal customers, not to mention rich sources of referral. Does it always happen that way? Well, not always, but it *never* happens if you walk away from a marketing campaign before it has a chance to come to life.

Maintaining commitment in the face of everything requires that you consider the following:

- If you are tempted to drop it, think of how much money you invested in producing it—along with your investments of time, energy, imagination, and information.
- If you are tempted to drop it, think of how much money you invested in building awareness of your brand, money and awareness that now floats into nothingness on wings of impatience.
- If you are tempted to drop it because you feel that such an act will save you money, know that is just like stopping your wristwatch in the hopes of saving time.
- If you are tempted to drop it because it did not produce instant results, realize that it is not supposed to produce instant results. Guerrilla marketing is supposed to produce eventual and permanent results. It is supposed to attract the most loyal and knowledgeable customers. It is supposed to result in measurable profits that grow with the same consistency as your marketing exposure. It is not supposed to produce instant results.

Admittedly, there are several kinds of marketing, usually centered around sales, discounts, and Wal-Mart type operations, that do produce instant results. But if that's the kind of marketing you want, we hope you get yourself another guerrilla. That kind of marketing either requires a multibillion dollar unheralded relationship with not a company but a nation like China, or it attracts the worst kind of customers, disloyal enough to be won over only by price, then won by another and still another price. Hardly the basis for a long-term profitable business. If it's the strategy you pursue during the start-up phase of your guerrilla marketing, we caution you with red flags waving that you may be starting in the wrong direction.

Maintaining a guerrilla marketing attack means being impervious to the usual distractions. The natural forces of the universe, time and human nature, are on your side. With time, your brand becomes better known and more trusted. With human nature, your commitment to your brand becomes more apparent, making those humans more confident in your business. And what's the number-one reason that people patronize a business? Confidence in that business.

The great brands in history, from Coca-Cola to McDonald's, from Marlboro to Metropolitan Life, were not instant successes. Heck it even took the zipper over 40 years to be accepted by a zipperless public! You can be sure that the leaders of all those brands at one time or another felt like throwing in the towel. But as with you, the decision to press on resided with them. They made the tough decision. It's one that might be facing you, too. Maintaining the attack goes on today as it started to the day they opened their doors. Everyone falls down 10 times. Winners get up 11.

> *We hate to admit this in public, but . . . "mediocre marketing with commitment is far better than brilliant marketing without it."*

The 17 Secrets of Guerrilla Marketing That Help You Maintain Your Attack

The concepts below are probably the reason that many start-up guerrillas now run highly successful companies. They are the cornerstones of guerrilla marketing. These are not just 17 words. Each one is nuclear-powered and capable of propelling you into the land of your dreams if you memorize them and operate your business by the concepts that they represent. They also come with a handy memory crutch. Each word ends with the letters ENT. They are:

1. *Commitment.* You should know that a mediocre marketing program with commitment will always prove more profitable than a brilliant marketing program without commitment. Commitment makes it happen.

2. *Investment.* Marketing is not an expense, but an investment—the best investment available in America today if you do it right. With the secrets of guerrilla marketing to guide you, you'll be doing it right.

3. *Consistent.* It takes a while for prospects to trust you, and if you change your marketing, media, and identity, you're hard to trust. Restraint is a great ally of the guerrilla. Repetition is another.

4. *Confident.* In a nationwide test to determine why people buy, price came in fifth, selection fourth, service third, and quality second. In first place was confident. People said they patronize businesses in which they are confident.

5. *Patient.* Unless the person running your marketing is patient, it will be difficult to practice commitment, view marketing as an investment, be consistent, and make prospects confident. Patience is a guerrilla virtue.

6. *Assortment.* Guerrillas know that individual marketing weapons rarely work on their own. However, marketing combinations *do*

work. A wide assortment of marketing tools is required to woo and win customers.

7. *Convenient.* People now know that time is not money, but is far more valuable than money. Respect this by being easy to do business with and running your company for the convenience of your customers, not yourself.

8. *Subsequent.* The real profits come after you've made the sale, in the form of repeat and referral business. Nonguerrillas think marketing ends when they've made the sale. Guerrillas know that's when marketing begins.

9. *Amazement.* There are elements of your business that you take for granted, but prospects would be amazed if they knew the details. Be sure all of your marketing always reflects that amazement. It's always there. Marketing creativity is the truth made fascinating.

10. *Measurement.* You can actually double your profits by measuring the results of your marketing. Some weapons hit bulls-eyes. Others miss the target. Unless you measure, you won't know which are which.

11. *Involvement.* This describes the relationship between you and your customers—and it is a relationship. You prove your involvement by following up; they prove theirs by patronizing and recommending you.

12. *Dependent.* The guerrilla's job is not to compete with but to cooperate with other businesses. Market them in return for their marketing you. Set up tie-ins with others. Become dependent to market more and invest less.

13. *Armament.* Armament is defined as "the equipment necessary to wage and win battles." The armament of guerrillas is technology: computers, current software, cell phones, pagers, and

fax machines. Remember, if you're technophobic, see a technoshrink.

14. *Consent*. In an era of nonstop interruption marketing, the key to success is to first gain consent to receive your marketing materials, then market only to those who have given you that consent. Don't waste money on people who don't give consent to you.

15. *Content*. Sell the content of your offering rather than the style. Sell the sizzle and the steak because people are too sophisticated to merely buy that sizzle.

16. *Augment*. For example, to succeed online, augment your web site with offline promotions, constant maintenance of your site, participation in newsgroups and forums, e-mail, chatroom attendance, posted articles, conference hosting, and rapid follow up.

17. *Implement*. As we have reminded you previously, guerrilla marketing is definitely not a spectator sport. Everything that you have been learning in this book must be converted into action to become a successful guerrilla entrepreneur.

19

KEEPING TRACK

This is the part where you really get it about commitment. This is the part where you learn the significance of keeping good records. With records, you know which marketing succeeded and which failed. Without them, it's just another period of groping and praying, which has not proven to be the right approach.

You're in your regular business, but you're also in the marketing business. People in that business think that marketing is about groping and praying. Too few know that it's about keeping records, making decisions based upon hard facts, and then keeping more records because you also get it about maintaining your attack. Let us tell you something about marketing: It's a world of uncertainty. It's not a barrel of fun knowing you'll probably be wrong half the time—or more. Ouch.

We've included this chapter on keeping track to relieve your pain. Because if you keep track, you emerge from that world of uncertainty and move onto solid ground. Once you realize that you can run your business on facts and truths instead of feelings and instincts, the whole idea of earning profits comes into clear view.

It is important that you train all your employees to ask every customer, "How did you hear about us?" Ask the customer to be specific. Was it our billboard? Our newspaper ad? Our radio spot? Our TV commercial? As you experiment with different marketing weapons, this information will be crucial to keep track of so that you will know your bull's-eyes from your misses. This will also help you in grading your guerrilla marketing calendar and in making out a new one the following year.

You can sense the confidence and victory that comes from knowing things for certain. Here's the best part: The more and the better you keep track, the better equipped you'll be to attack and defend in

TESTING, TESTING

Naturally, you must test all of your communications. Place the same ad in two publications. If one outpulls another, as you hope, eliminate the losing publication and begin to go deep with the better ad. Test ad sizes, colors, timing, and headlines.

Once you've got a bead on those elements of the creative process, begin sharpening your copy, testing one version against another, and after that—because you don't want to test more than one thing at a time—test your graphics. Photograph or illustration? Keep track of the results to get the right answer. Don't go with your guts, enticing as that may sound. This truly is the time to give that adage a rest, and use the economy and ease of the internet to give you facts where you once relied on courage. General Custer relied on courage.

the present and future. The more hard information you have about your marketing, your competitors, your industry, the world economy, psychology, the media, the internet, communications technology, and your customers, the more profits you'll earn. It's not necessarily easy, but it's indisputably certain.

Initially, keeping track alerts you to islands of solid ground on the sink-or-swim marketing terrain, but eventually, due in large part to your newfound penchant for keeping track, you'll locate more solid ground and more higher ground. You breathe easier because you can sense the certainty in the air. Where there used to be chaos, now there is order. It didn't happen by accident. It happened because you began learning what to keep track of.

Many people think that marketing is a glamor business. In many cases, they are right. Dealing with creative types is glamorous. It's the same with dealing with producers and directors and writers and consummate professionals in the fields of research and media. But keeping track of a marketing attack is decidedly not glamorous, except for the bank deposits that will result from your assiduousness. The same is true about maintaining an attack. It's about as glamorous as getting 40 lashes.

Keeping track is the medicine that keeps the pain at bay. Keeping track is the illumination that shows you the way. Keeping track improves your vision so that you see more clearly and distantly than your competitors. Some of them keep track, too. But do they keep track of as many factors influencing a sale? Do they analyze those factors, then act upon what they learned?

Keeping track is one of the most expeditious ways to save money because it reveals so openly the flaws in a campaign. That means you can save about 50 percent of your financial investment in marketing. Are we kidding you here? Fifty percent of your financial investment? We kid you not. Do the math. You have two ads, or brochures, or web sites, or commercials, or e-mails. One will probably test better, which means one will earn more profits for you than the other. The math

> Keeping track is the medicine that keeps the pain at bay. Keeping track is the illumination that shows you the way. Keeping track improves your vision so that you see more clearly and distantly than your competitors.

> Keeping track is one of the most expeditious ways to save money because it reveals so openly the flaws in a campaign.

> Keeping track is contributing to your momentum by directing you to the winners only and by eliminating the losers.

might not always come to a 50 percent savings, but it always points out that one is a loser and another is a winner. Keeping track is contributing to your momentum by directing you to the winners only and by eliminating the losers.

Of course, the most important thing to keep track of is the profitability of your marketing. If one ad beats the stuffing out of another ad, that doesn't mean it's a good ad. Does it generate profits for your company? If it does, then it's a good ad. But can it be made better? Probably. Why not test it against another version to see which generates the highest profits? That is precisely what we'll look into in the next chapter.

20

IMPROVING YOUR MARKETING

In real estate, the three biggest secrets of success are location, location, and location. The three biggest in marketing are test, test, and test. Of the many ways to improve your marketing, testing ranks at the top. No matter how wonderful you think a web site, an ad, or a headline might be, there's a good chance that testing can prove you wrong. And that's a good thing. The last thing you want is to commit to a subpar marketing message.

When you set out to improve your marketing, that means improving your

- headline,
- subhead,
- copy,
- offer,
- price,

In real estate, the three biggest secrets of success are location, location, and location. The three biggest in marketing are test, test, and test.

- graphics,
- typography,
- media,
- mailing list,
- web site,
- brand identity,
- response rates,
- hits,
- conversion rate, and
- profits.

Although it's listed last here, improving your profits is the reason you make any of these marketing improvements in the first place. All of the areas requiring improvement are areas that when improved will improve your bottom line.

Just how do you go about improving in all of those areas? You know how: testing. Test those areas. Once you've got a winner, test again to beat the winner. Pretty soon, you'll have a bead on what works with your audience and what doesn't. That's why it's crucial that you continue zeroing in on that audience so that you can get to the core of it and find more people just like your customers. As you do these things, your taste and judgement will improve on a regular basis.

Unlike many of the other facets of marketing, the process of testing should never end. You should constantly strive to improve upon your highest test scores and best response rates. Always keep in mind that as you improve your marketing, the scorekeeper is your profit and loss statement.

Always keep in mind that as you improve your marketing, the scorekeeper is your profit and loss statement.

Once you have a campaign, e-mail, or ad that works well for you, keep running it. Do not be self-conscious about how many times that may be. With your scorekeeper and bottom line being one and the same, you should have no trouble staying the course. Repetition is a very powerful ally because it enables you to run the same campaign while improving the results you get from each of the components of the campaign. Many misguided marketers have the mistaken notion that their marketing is supposed to change regularly. That kind of thinking puts a hole in even the deepest pockets. The idea is to get it right then stay with it.

One of the most winning aspects of the internet is the economy that it offers to guerrillas who seek to improve their marketing. You can make an offer on your web site today, then make a different offer tomorrow, and a still different offer the day after tomorrow. The cost of changing your offers is nil. You enjoy the same economy with e-mail and can test your way to certainty at little or no cost. The major media cannot offer such speed or economy.

While you are running your marketing campaign, you can be testing your marketing with small sample mailings all along, attempting to improve your marketing as you run it. In big companies, there is constant testing, constant improving, constant tweaking. There can be the same degree of experimentation in your company. Size doesn't matter.

A good reason to consistently improve your marketing is that your competitors will begin to copy you. Sure, imitation is the sincerest form of flattery, and the imitator will be reminding people of your company as they copy you. But if you are improving your campaign as you run it, they'll be very hardpressed to keep up with you.

We realize that it's a long journey to that place where you can count on your marketing doing the job for you and count on the profits you are certain to earn as a result of all your hard work. Just when you expect us to give you a high five and a congratulatory pat on the back, here we are advising you to continue improving your marketing campaign. Get your congratulations from the increased profits you'll be enjoying.

Is there ever a time you can just kick back and let your marketing do all the heavy lifting for you? The answer is a resounding no, unless your competitors are all doing the same. And you know they won't. So you can't. Guerrillas set a blistering pace, then shift into another gear and pick up the pace even more.

> Many misguided marketers have the mistaken notion that their marketing is supposed to change regularly. That kind of thinking puts a hole in even the deepest pockets. The idea is to get it right then stay with it.

A word of warning: Be prepared to get egg on your face. As you constantly test new ideas, you've got to take chances with some of your experimenting. You can't always take the safe route. You've got to venture into uncharted territory and risk being wrong. We know a company president who is always testing five new approaches—and one of them is always a real off-the-wall brainstorm. Some of those wild new approaches get embarrassingly low test scores, but occasionally, one of them doubles the previous response rate and sends the profits soaring.

Your profits, sales, and marketing insight will improve, and you may feel as though you have achieved the right level of success with marketing. That will probably be true. But also true is the reality that your competitors will be keeping their eyes on you. Their profits, sales, and marketing insight will also get better. They'll be learning by watching and spying on you, as well as by reading some of the brilliant books about marketing, attending the marketing seminars that are becoming more helpful and more popular, and observing the marketing activities in their industry, community, and latest trade publications.

TWO SCHOOLS

Enroll in two schools at the same time: The school that teaches you that looking at the big picture gives you the clearest perspective and the school that specializes in teaching that the smaller the picture you study, the more you'll learn.

There was a professor in college at the University of Colorado. One day he took the class outside and we studied a single flower for a full hour. It's hard to imagine learning more about botany.

Which school are you, the start-up guerrilla, supposed to choose for your curriculum? It's obvious that you'll have to choose both.

Don't think of it as a battle. Instead, think of it as natural evolution. Survival of the fittest seems especially pertinent in the world of small business, where glaring errors cannot be obfuscated by millions of dollars. The more deeply involved you become in the marketing process, the more you'll sense that your marketing program has to be flexible because of the speed of change. You still must commit to it, but you can and should make rare changes when you think they are necessary. Putting it all together begins *after* you've made your initial adjustments. The process of starting up with guerrilla marketing begins when you think the animal through.

You don't want to risk obliviousness to the big picture. You dare not conduct your marketing without knowing exactly what's going on in the small picture. With knowledge comes improvement. Amen.

PUTTING IT
ALL TOGETHER

As we wind down the act of winding you up, we look back and see that you've already attended to the origin of your guerrilla marketing effort, actually started your momentum. You've investigated and grown to know the core guerrilla within you and what you must do to make him or her the perfect guerrilla.

You've learned the specific attributes and company attitudes that will speed you toward the deposit window—or your computer. Although it is not their favorite activity, guerrillas do their banking online because of the need to keep records and to save time. They use the internet whenever they can, but certainly not all the time. They are decidedly not scared or intimated by computers. They realize that it's the place where the marketing struggles take place and where victories can be assured. We ask, "Where does it all come together?" And we answer, "At the computer."

> Not knowing how to use a keyboard in the 21st century is akin to not knowing how to use a telephone in the 20th century.

To be a rip-roaring success with guerrilla marketing, along with your prime investments of time, energy, imagination, and information your cause will be aided immensely if you are computer savvy, if you are a good writer, and if you're a fast typist. Not knowing how to use a keyboard in the 21st century is akin to not knowing how to use a telephone in the 20th century.

We shouldn't have to mention this, but after witnessing many failures who lacked a powerful work ethic, I'm compelled to reveal that if you don't really have one, you should do something else for a living. Guerrilla marketing is not a get-rich-quick scheme. It's a get-rich-eventually scheme.

Knowing about guerrilla marketing, as you do, is still not enough. You've got to do it right. You can't put up a blog and make entries into it every two weeks. You can't put up a web site, then unintentionally hide the benefits it bestows on visitors.

COMPUTERS HELP GUERRILLAS IN FIVE INVALUABLE WAYS

1. By giving them the opportunity to put up a web site.

2. By making it simple and free to use e-mail.

3. By giving them access to the information superhighway in the form of a vast treasury of righteous data.

4. By allowing them to spy closely on their competitors.

5. By granting them the economic and profit-producing advantages of desktop publishing. Don't get us started on desktop publishing. It's a mandatory capability for owners of small businesses.

There's no question that you know the ten steps you must take to hit it out of the park with your guerrilla marketing assault. We're confident that you won't shortchange yourself while taking those ten steps, but frankly, we do worry about your ability to maintain the attack in the face of consumer rejection or worse still, apathy. Consumer rejection is simply an indication that you can ask questions all the way to the close of the sale. Ask what you could have done to win their business. Ask questions all the way to the close, and listen carefully to their answers. Rejection is nearly as good as acceptance in the minds of guerrilla marketers. Apathy is a different critter. It's a critter who doesn't even know you're around, so you certainly can't ask questions.

Faced with such dire circumstances, will you be able to maintain your attack? If you remember that falling short of your dreams initially was likely to happen, you won't feel quite as frustrated. If you recall that premature abandonment is the biggest error made in small business marketing, you won't be in such a hurry to abandon your campaign. When sales and profits fall short of your justifiably optimistic projections, repeat these words to yourself: commitment, commitment, commitment. There. That'll do it. That, plus time.

> Premature abandonment is the biggest error made in small business marketing.

Putting it all together means crafting a guerrilla marketing campaign, breathing life into it the right way, keeping track of its effects, and sticking with it while it's just a little baby. That's the time it's going to need you the most, certainly no time for you to tiptoe off in the night to another guerrilla. Save your talent and energy, save your money and your resources for improving your attack—later.

> **General George Patton said, "A pretty good plan executed today is better than a perfect plan executed tomorrow."**

As a side note, although we have told you all about guerrilla marketing, in reality, we must remind you that sometimes an increase business profits has more to do with the use of simple common sense, and nothing to do with marketing of any kind. The story below illustrates this point.

SIMPLE CHANGES

There is a large well-known hot sauce company whose profit level had started to plateau. The CEO of the company decided to call a meeting with its advertising department, online department, and PR department. He asked each one of them if he budgeted a million dollars to their department, how would they spend the money to increase their profits. He told them to each come back in a month to present their proposals.

A month went by, and the meeting was about to convene. On the way to the board room, the CEO spotted a new hire, a young girl fresh out of college, and asked her to join the meeting. She was taken aback as she had only been working there a few weeks. The CEO told her he wanted her to sit in the meeting just so that she could get a feel for how big business works.

At the meeting each department presented its proposal on how it would invest a million dollars into its marketing. When they were done, the CEO looked at the young girl, and asked, "If you were me, what would you do?" The girl said, "May I speak frankly?" "Of course," answered the CEO. "If it were my decision," she replied, "I would just make the holes in the top of the bottles a little bit larger."

The CEO decided to take her advice, and company profits went up 7 percent the first year, and 14 percent the following year. As a matter of fact, it has had an increase in sales every year ever since, and it didn't spend an extra penny in marketing.

As you can see, it is important to note as you are working on increasing your own profits, that you also must consider that a healthy dose of pure common sense can go along way.

Now that you've learned all of these guerrilla marketing strategies and tactics to run your business successfully, there is yet another side to this guerrilla coin—learning to practice balance and harmony to be successful in life. The following are excerpts taken from our book *The Guerrilla Entrepreneur* (Morgan James Publishing, 2007) formerly titled *The Way of the Guerrilla*.

The goals of the 21st century guerrilla entrepreneur: work that is satisfying, enough money to enjoy freedom from worry about it, health good enough to take for granted, a bonding with others where you give and receive love and support, fun that is not pursued but is in the essence of daily living, and longevity to appreciate with wisdom what you have achieved.

What Is a Guerrilla Entrepreneur?

The guerrilla entrepreneur knows that the journey is the goal. He also realizes that he is in control of his enterprise, not the other way around, and that if he is dissatisfied with his journey, he is missing the point of the journey itself. Unlike old-fashioned enterprises, which often required gigantic sacrifices for the sake of the goal, guerrilla enterprises place the goal of a pleasant journey ahead of the mere notion of sacrifices.

The guerrilla entrepreneur achieves balance from the very start. He builds free time into his work schedule so that balance is part of his enterprise. He respects his leisure time as much as his work time, never allowing too much of one to interfere with the other. Traditional entrepreneurs always placed work ahead of leisure and showed no respect for their own personal freedom. Guerrillas cherish their freedom as much as their work.

The guerrilla entrepreneur is not in a hurry. A false need for speed frequently undermines even the best-conceived strategies. Haste makes waste and sacrifices quality. The guerrilla is fully aware that patience is his ally, and he has planned intelligently to eliminate most emergencies that call for moving fast. His pace is always steady but never rushed.

The guerrilla entrepreneur uses stress as a benchmark. If he feels any stress, he knows he must be going about things in the wrong way. Guerrilla entrepreneurs do not accept stress as part of doing business and recognize any stress as a warning sign that something's the matter—in the work plan of the guerrilla or in the business itself. Adjustments are made to eliminate the cause of the stress rather than the stress itself.

The guerrilla entrepreneur looks forward to work. He has a love affair with his work and considers himself blessed to be paid for doing the work he does. He is good at his work, energizing his passion for it in a quest to learn more about it and improve his understanding of it, thereby increasing his skills. The guerrilla entrepreneur doesn't think about retirement, for never would he want to stop doing work he loves.

The guerrilla entrepreneur has no weaknesses. He is effective in every aspect of his enterprise because he has filled in the gaps between his strengths and talents with people who abound in the prowess he lacks. He is very much the team player and teams up with guerrillas like himself who share the team spirit and possess complementary skills. He values his teammates as much as old-fashioned entrepreneurs valued their independence.

The guerrilla entrepreneur is fusion oriented. He is always on the alert to fuse his business with other enterprises in town, in America, in the world. He is willing to combine marketing efforts, production skills, information, leads, mailing lists, and anything else to increase his effectiveness and marketing reach while reducing the cost of achieving those goals. His fusion efforts are intentionally short term and rarely permanent. In his business relationships, instead of thinking marriage, he thinks fling.

The guerrilla entrepreneur does not kid himself. He knows that if he over-estimates his own abilities, he runs the risk of skimping on the quality he represents to his customers, employees, investors, suppliers, and fusion partners. He forces himself to face reality on a daily basis and realizes that all of his business practices must always be evaluated in the glaring light of what is really happening, instead of what should be happening.

The guerrilla entrepreneur lives in the present. He is well aware of the past, very enticed by the future, but the here and now is where he resides, embracing the technologies of the present, leaving future technologies on the horizon right where they belong—on the horizon until later when they are ripe and ready. He is alert to the new, wary of the avante-garde, and only wooed from the old by improvement, not merely change.

The guerrilla entrepreneur understands the precious nature of time. He doesn't buy into the old lie that time is money and knows in his heart that time is far more important than money. He knows that instead, time is *life*. He is aware that his customers and prospects feel the same way about time, so he respects theirs and wouldn't dare waste it. As a practicing guerrilla, he is the epitome of efficiency but never lets it interfere with his effectiveness.

The guerrilla entrepreneur always operates according to a plan. He knows who he is, where he is going, and how he will get there. He is prepared, knows that anything can and will happen, and can deal with the barriers to entrepreneurial success because his plan has foreseen them and shown exactly how to surmount them. The guerrilla reevaluates his plan regularly and does not hesitate to make changes in it, though commitment to the plan is part of his very being.

The guerrilla entrepreneur is flexible. He is guided by a strategy for success, and knows the difference between a guide and a master. When it is necessary to change, the guerrilla changes, accepting change as part of the status quo, not ignoring or battling it. He is able to adapt to new situations, realizes that service is whatever his customers want it to be, and knows that inflexible things become brittle and break.

The guerrilla aims for results more than growth. He is focused upon profitability and balance, vitality and improvement, and value and quality more than size and growth. His plan calls for steadily increasing profits without a sacrifice of personal time, so his actions are oriented to hitting those targets instead of growing for the sake of growth alone. He is wary of becoming large and does not equate hugeness with excellence.

The guerrilla entrepreneur is dependent upon many people. He knows that the age of the lone wolf entrepreneur, independent and proud of it, has passed. The guerrilla is very dependent upon his fusion business partners, his employees, his customers, his suppliers, and his mentors. He got where he is with his own wings, his own determination, his own smarts, and as a guerrilla, with a little help from a lot of friends.

The guerrilla entrepreneur is constantly learning. A seagull flies in circles in the sky, looking for food in an endless quest. When it finally finds the food, the seagull lands and eats its fill. When it has completed its meal, the seagull returns to the sky, only to fly in circles again, searching for food even though it has just eaten. Humans have only one instinct that compares: the need for constant learning. Guerrilla entrepreneurs have this need in spades.

The guerrilla entrepreneur is passionate about work. He has an enthusiasm for what he does that is apparent to everyone who sees his work. This enthusiasm spreads to everyone who works with him, even to his customers. In its purest form, this enthusiasm is best expressed as the word: passion—an intense feeling that burns within him and is manifested in the devotion he demonstrates toward his business.

The guerrilla entrepreneur is focused on the goal. He knows that balance does not come easily and that he must rid himself of the values and expectations of his ancestors. To do this, he must remain focused upon his journey, seeing the future clearly while at the same time concentrating upon the present. He is aware that the minutiae of life and business can distract him, so he does what is necessary to make those distractions only momentary.

The guerrilla entrepreneur is disciplined about the tasks at hand. He is keenly aware that every time he writes a task on his daily calendar, it is a promise he is making to himself. As a guerrilla who does not kid himself, he keeps those promises, knowing that the achievement of

TEN DIRTY LIES YOU HAVE KNOWN AND LOVED

1. Time is money.
2. Owning a business means workaholism.
3. Marketing is expensive.
4. Big corporations are like wombs.
5. Youth is better than age.
6. You need a job.
7. Heaven is in the afterlife.
8. The purpose of education is to teach facts.
9. Retirement is a good thing.
10. If you want it done right, do it yourself.

his goals will be a more than adequate reward for his discipline. He finds it easy to be disciplined because of the payback offered by the leisure that follows.

The guerrilla entrepreneur is well-organized at home and at work. He does not waste valuable time looking for items that have been misplaced, so he organizes as he works and as new work comes to him. His sense of organization is fueled by the efficiency that results from it. While he is always organized, the guerrilla never squanders precious time by overorganizing.

The guerrilla entrepreneur has an upbeat attitude. Because he knows that life is unfair, problems arise, to err is human, and the cool shall inherit the Earth, he manages to take obstacles in stride, keeping his perspective and his sense of humor. His ever-present optimism is grounded in an ability to perceive the positive side of things, recognizing the negative but never dwelling there. His positivity is contagious.

Business in the New Millennium

Two things you can be very certain about in the 21st century are that business will be a lot harder and that business will be a lot easier. It will be harder because of five factors:

1. *Time.* Time will be magnified in importance. The luxury of spare time at work is a luxury of the past. Spare time will be revered, but not at work. You will be unable to help but notice the new awareness of time by almost everyone. Customers will demand and expect speed. You will, too.

2. *Contact.* Less face-to-face contact will remove much of the warmth of working. People now get over half their messages by non-verbal communication. This means that nonverbal communications will be less accurate; verbal accuracy more valuable. The joy of social interaction will be much abated.

3. *Change.* Change will be thrust upon us, and much that we counted on before will no longer hold true. Even things we learn will only be true for a short time before being surpassed by new truths. The genius will not be in learning something but in learning one thing after another. If you can't adapt, you aren't cut out to be a guerrilla.

4. *Talent.* Talent will be diffuse as top people trade the vitality of a huge corporation for the tranquillity of working at home. Well and good for them, but for guerrilla entrepreneurs, this means all the big brains won't be under one roof. You'll have to scout them out.

5. *Technology.* Technology will be more important in your life, and you'll have to understand it to take full advantage of it. But technical things are becoming easier to use, user manuals are written more clearly, and the nature of training (repetition will be your friend for life) has improved. As we said before, if you're technophobic, see a technoshrink.

The five ways that business will be easier are really 5,000 ways, but for purposes of time let's just go with five right here:

1. *Time.* You will have more time to do what really must be done rather than just doing busywork, because technical advancements will allow it. Your network of independent contractors will also free up more of your time. Use the time to increase your profits, make your business better, or just plain enjoy yourself.

2. *Values.* Values will change and they will be more in keeping with your own guerrilla values. In the 20th century, the main value was placed on making money. In the 21st century, that priority will take a back seat to the human values of happiness at work, free time, family, and spirituality. As you are discovering, profit seeking will never be eliminated, only reprioritized.

3. *Advancements.* New advancements in business, both psychological and technological, will make the workplace more exciting

and easier to use, even enjoyable. Flex-time and tele-conferencing will make for less crowded commuting if you commute at all. The virtual office is the at-home office. And it's here now.

4. *Procedures*. Streamlined procedures will keep your work life efficient, organized, simple, and fast. You won't waste time or effort at work because you'll have learned to become an efficient working machine, and as a guerrilla entrepreneur, you'll realize that the whole purpose of streamlining is to add *effectiveness*.

5. *People*. You will deal with smarter people, and they'll be fewer in number. Your workplace won't be populated with paper-shufflers. Your at-home business will put you into contact with bright, talented entrepreneurs who made the break from the corporate life and are doing very well, just like you.

The Pitfalls of Being an Entrepreneur

There are drawbacks to being an entrepreneur, but if you are aware of them, you have the chance to avoid letting them control your life. Here they are.

Pitfall 1: The Time Trap

As much as people revere leisure time, they have less of it than ever, averaging 32 percent less leisure time than they had in the 1980s. Here I am jumping up and glorifying the three-day week when increasing numbers of Americans are wondering how to get out from under the six-day week. Habits are much easier to form than they are to break. "I'll just work 60 hours a week for now, and then I'll cut back later." Won't happen.

Pitfall 2: The Large Lure

You'll be offered chances to earn more money, expand, take on more people, move to a larger space, and transform from an entrepreneurial endeavor to a large corporate-type entity. Hey, it's your life, but you've got to turn in your guerrilla credentials if you opt for large rather than free, for bigness over balance.

Pitfall 3: The Money Morass

Money alters human behavior to the point that it causes well-meaning owners of small business who are bound for success to veer in the direction of financial success, steamrollering any chances of emotional, marital, parental, or social success. Money, being easier to attain than balance, is more frequently sought. Those in pursuit of it find that the prices they pay are worth far more than money. Of all the pitfalls, the money morass is the deepest, darkest, and biggest.

Pitfall 4: The Burnout Barrier

You'll search your soul to come up with a method for providing your livelihood and you'll set up shop with all the right intentions. You'll work hard and smart, and your rewards will be fruitful. But somewhere along the way, you lose some of your initial enthusiasm for your work. You'll continue on because you've been successful, but you'll bring less and less joy to your work. The thrill is gone. There is no more enthusiasm. You burned out. What to do now is *something else*. If the spark is gone, get yourself another dream. Enthusiasm will fuel your fires, and if it is absent, the fire in your soul will go out—the fire that was the key to your success. Guerrillas know that they can relight the fire for a new venture and that studies prove that the more you love what you do, the better you'll do it. So if you no longer feel the love, end the relationship and start another.

Pitfall 5: The Humanity Hindrance

We hope like crazy that you never lose your personal warmth, your sense of humor, or your love of other human beings in your quest to become a successful entrepreneur. Sadly, the world has more than enough tales of individuals who left a trail of shattered people on their climb to the top. The guerrilla's priority list places people ahead of business, family ahead of business, love ahead of business, and self ahead of business. Keeping your eyes on the bottom line should not make them beady. Putting your heart in your work should not turn it to stone. Attaining everything on your wish list should not put you upon anybody's enemy list. An executive I knew at a *Fortune* 500 company had a glass eye. When I asked which was the glass eye, I was told, "It's the warm one." There is no rule that says you give up your humanity as the dues for achieving entrepreneurial success.

Pitfall 6: The Focus Foil

It is not difficult to lose your focus and set it upon a false goal, a tangential journey leading away from your dreams. You become so involved in the details of your operation that you deviate from your prime thrust. Your time becomes gobbled up by details instead of broad strokes. The idea is to grow your mind as your grow your business but still maintain your direction.

Pitfall 7: The Perfection Pit

High atop our own list of time-wasters, life-stealers, and company-ruiners are perfectionists and the pursuit of perfection. I am all for excellence and admire perfection in a bowling game or classroom attendance—two areas where perfection is possible. Guerrillas try to be perfect, but don't spend all their time and energy attaining it. They know that the world is teeming with entrepreneurs who spend half their time polishing the unpolishable, steeped in the unnecessary, devoted to the unattainable. May your enterprise be free from imperfections and from perfectionists.

Pitfall 8: The Selling Snare

The selling snare is a trap that forces you to sell the same thing over and over again. The guerrilla's way around it: *Make multiple sales with one effort.* Instead of selling a single issue of a magazine, sell a subscription. Guerrillas do all in their power to develop products or services that must be purchased on a regular basis. Many offerings are sold with the repeat sales built right in, from our *Guerrilla Marketing Newsletter* to cable television, from cleaning services to diaper service, from insurance coverage to gardening, from swimming pool maintenance to dental care. The idea is to apply the ultimate in selling skills so that your one-time sale can lead to years and year of profits. If you fall into the trap of selling single shots only, you'll be spending more time selling than enjoying the benefits of your efforts.

Pitfall 9: The Leisure Lure

Don't kid yourself into believing that leisure time is automatically a good thing. Leisure time when you don't know what do to with it can lead to a wide variety of problems—from boredom to substance abuse. Truth be told, many people actually enjoy their work time more than their leisure time because at least they know what they'll be doing with their work time. They haven't a clue as to how to spend their leisure hours. Guerrillas do have a clue. And a hobby. And a slew of interests beyond working and earning money. They enjoy their leisure almost as much as their work because they are working at something they love and because they've given a lot of thought to what they'll do with their free time. They know that free time without focus can be a drag.

Pitfall 10: The Retirement Ruse

Horrid but true: More than 75 percent of retirees die within two years of their retirement. When they retire from work, it's as though they also retire from life. Don't make the mistake of planning for retirement. Plan on cutting down, on easing off, but not on quitting altogether.

Working keeps you sharp, keeps your brain in shape. Ceasing to work allows your brain to atrophy. What are most retirees concerned with? Well, 38 percent say they don't have enough money. Another 29 percent say they're fearful of not staying healthy. Eight percent say they have too much time on their hands and they're bored. And eight percent figure they probably won't live long enough to enjoy life.

Guerrillas have enough money because they put retirement into the same category as imprisonment. The money continues to flow into their lives long after their cohorts have retired. They stay healthy because continuing to hone the edge caused by work results in the maintenance of health and increased longevity. They do not suffer from the problem of too much time, having just enough for work, and just enough for play. And they have been enjoying life all along because they've been engaged in the work they love, a trademark of the guerrilla entrepreneur.

In nature, nothing ever retires, and as we are getting closer to understanding our own relationship with nature, we are understanding that retirement is unhealthy and contraindicated in anyone with brain waves. As an entrepreneur, you are your own boss. No one is going to *make* you retire.

What happens if you are simply no longer interested in the business? Retire from it—then move on to another dream. Just don't retire from life itself. The trap of planning for retirement is like planning your own slow suicide, brought upon by inactivity.

Just Being a Guerrilla Gives You an Edge

You've got the guerrilla's edge in *insight*. You've given thought to your priorities. You aren't going to be misled by entrepreneurial myths involving overwork, overgrowth, and overextending your reach. You realize that your journey is your destination and that your plan is your road map. This insight will help you maintain your passion.

You've got the guerrilla's edge in *relationships*. Every sale you make leads to a lasting relationship. Every customer you get is going to be a customer for life. Your sales and even your profits will probably go up and down, but your number of relationships will constantly go up, and your sales and profits will eventually follow.

You've got the guerrilla's edge in *service*. You see your service from your customer's point of view, not merely from your own. You realize that your service gives you an enormous competitive advantage over those who may be larger but less devoted to making and keeping customers delighted with your company. You know well the power of word-of-mouth marketing and how it equates with excellent service.

You've got the guerrilla's edge in *flexibility*. You are not enslaved by company policies and by precedent. Instead, you are fast on your feet, sensitive to customer needs, and aware of flexibility as a tool for building relationships, profits, and your overall company. You are guided by the situation at hand and not by the way things were done in the past. Your flexibility adds to the passion that others feel about your company.

You've got the guerrilla's edge in *follow-up*. You don't have to be reminded about the number of potential relationships that are destroyed by customers being ignored after they made a purchase. Rather than ignoring them, you pay attention to them, remind them of how glad you are that they're customers, and pepper them with special offers, inside information, and care. They never feel ignored by you and reciprocate by never ignoring your company when it comes to repeat purchases or referrals.

You have the guerrilla's edge in *cooperation*. You see other businesses as potential partners of yours, as firms that can help you as you help them. You don't keep your eye peeled for competitors to annihilate but for businesses to team up with and form networks with. Your attitude will help you prosper in an era when people are forming small businesses in droves.

You have the guerrilla's edge in *patience*. As a guerrilla, you are not in a hurry, never in a rush. You know how important time is, but you also know how speed usually results in diminished quality. Because of your planning, you are able to avoid emergencies and high-pressure situations. Patience is one of your staunchest allies as a guerrilla.

You have the guerrilla's edge in *economy*. You know how to market without investing a bundle of hard-earned money. You have learned the value of time and energy as substitutes for large budgets. You realize that in most business activities, you have a choice of any two of these three factors: speed, economy, and quality. You always opt for economy and quality. Your patience helps you economize.

You have the guerrilla's edge in *timeliness*. You run a streamlined operation, devoid of fluff or unnecessary work. Your comfort with technology allows you to operate at maximum effectiveness. Your business is a state-of-the-art enterprise because it operates in the environment of today rather than ten years ago. Although you maintain your focus upon your plan, you know the magic of proper timing and are able to make adjustments so that you are there just when customers need you.

You have the guerrilla's edge in *commitment*. This commitment will set you apart from many other businesses. It will help you achieve your aims with certainty. It is so powerful that you feel passion towards the commitment itself—enabling the passion to power

LOVE IS THE KEY

1. Love of self
2. Love of work
3. Love of family
4. Love of play
5. Love of freedom

6. Love of independence
7. Love of friends
8. Love of customers and employees
9. Love of a higher power
10. Love of life

your commitment and the commitment to power your passion. Without this inner commitment, even the best plans may go awry. With it, plans turn into a bright reality.

The closer you examine it, the more you see that the way of the guerrilla is a way illuminated by the radiant light of *love*—love of self, work, family, others, freedom, independence, and life. The guerrilla has a lifelong love affair with life. The deeper and more heartfelt his love, the more he is capable of generating the fiery and exquisite passion that fuels his fires.

SUCCEEDING WITH
A GUERRILLA
MARKETING ATTACK

It's a jungle out there! You are surrounded. All around you are enemies vying for the same bounty. They're out to get your customers and your prospects, the good and honest people who ought to be buying what you are selling. These enemies are disguised as owners of small- and medium-sized businesses. Several of the enemies are grossly larger than you. Some have the power and personality of Godzilla. Many of them are far better funded than you. Some have been successfully operating their businesses since prehistoric times.

These enemies thrive on competition. They're out to get you and get you good. They're out for the disposable income currently held by your hot prospects and past customers. They're out for the attention of every red-blooded consumer who reads the newspaper, listens to the radio, watches TV, or grabs a handful of junk mail out of the mailbox.

Your enemies mean business: *your* business and *your* profits. Some of them can run more ads in more papers and more commercials on more stations than you'll ever run. They can mail more materials to more people than you'll ever mail. They can outspend you in every area of marketing that money can buy.

But they can't outspend you in areas that money can't buy. And they can't always out-think you—if you put up the time, the energy, the imagination, and the information.

The Ten-Step Attack Plan

Although planning, launching, fighting, and waging a successful guerrilla marketing attack can be the turning point for a company, as indeed it often is, remember it's only a ten-step process. Take those ten steps, not nine of them, and you'll bring in a lot of money, waste little, learn lifelong lessons, out-guerrilla your competition, and be poised to do it better the next time, no matter how well you did it this time.

All ten steps are easy to take, except one, and none take an especially long time, again with one exception. All are actually fun to do, except one. We discussed them in depth earlier, but now we summarize these steps to focus your mind. It's up to you to do a bang-up job. We're here to help but not to run into speeding locomotives for you

Step 1: All about Research

During this step, which doesn't take all that long, check out the overall scene. Check out the market, your product, affordable media, the competition, your industry, your prospects, your current customers, technology you might need, the benefits you offer, and for sure, the internet because you can learn so fast. This first step in your attack is a very long step, because you're not going to quit learning about your business for a long time.

At the beginning of a guerrilla marketing attack you are the most fascinating to your audience because they've never heard of you and

> Although planning, launching, fighting, and waging a successful guerrilla marketing attack can be the turning point for a company, as indeed it often is, it's only a ten-step process.

the most dangerous to your competitors because they don't know what to expect from you. But they do figure it's not going to help them.

Step 2: All about the Benefits You Offer

If ever there was a time to cast modesty to the winds, this is that time. Make a list of the good things that you offer to your clients or customers. Make it a long list. Invite friends and customers, relatives and acquaintances to solicit testimonials. That long list of benefits is just the start.

The next part is to face up to the fact that many of your competitors offer many of those same benefits. But . . . but . . . but . . .you probably offer benefits that your competition doesn't offer. Those are your competitive advantages. That's the fuel that powers your marketing machine.

Step 3: All about the Weapons You'll Use

If anyone knows weapons, it's you, so be prepared to inflict heavy profits on your company. Use them boldly. Use them confidently. Or stay away from them. With 200 weapons at your fingertips, we'd hate to be your competitors. The way to use the weapons you select is to remember that you're not firing all of them at the same time right at the beginning.

Make a list of the weapons you plan to use. List them in order: the first first, then second, then all the way to the last weapon you plan. Next to each weapon, pencil in a date and a person's initials. The date's your promised launch date and the person is the one who will take complete responsibililty for aiming and firing the weapon.

Step 4: All about Planning

This is the time for you to create that seven-sentence guerrilla marketing plan, but you've done yourself proud and completed it already. That's a powerful device you're holding—a device based on an idea. The device, a seven-sentence marketing plan, tells you what to do at the beginning and becomes more valuable with time because of the awesome power of commitment. Now you've got what it takes to have momentum.

Step 5: All about Your Marketing Calendar

We've already covered the guerrilla marketing calendar in great detail in Chapter 14. Use it as a road map to your success.

Step 6: All about Teamwork

The whole world is flourishing with bright, motivated, honest, high-energy people who would love to team up with you with the goal of three-way profit: you, the teammate, and the customer. These teammates exist in the form of affiliate partners, joint ventures, fusion marketing partners, co-marketers, licensees, and nameless and complex partnerships. They all stand for the same thing: They can help you make money if you help them make money. You put a discount coupon for them in your next e-mailing or paper mailing. They do the same for you the following week. Your back has been scratched and now you want to scratch someone else's back. Just google "affiliate marketing," then put in your order for that Rolls-Royce.

Step 7: All about Moving Slowly

The guerrilla moves quickly when the task demands, but life's pace for the guerrilla is slow. He launches his guerrilla marketing attack devastatingly, but not in a rush. Although his attack is broad and deep, he aims to feel comfort financially and emotionally, never investing too much and not having it eat into his time too much.

He's much more interested in learning the effect of his weaponry than in firing them himself. Guerrillas do not have trigger fingers. They'd probably lose the gunfight at the OK Corral. The guerrilla has learned that there are three factors in a marketing battle: speed, economy, and quality. He choses economy and quality every time. His planning has negated the need for speed.

Step 8: All about Maintaining the Attack

We've got to warn you, maintaining the attack is a bear of a step. Here's what's terrible about it:

- You're doing everything right and nothing is working.
- Your competitors are soaring ahead.
- Your investment in it seems embarrassingly misguided.
- The troops are grumbling—in the workplace and at home.
- The marketing experts are counseling you to mount a new and different marketing attack.

Think it's easy to withstand such a barrage of negativity? It is not, and that is why so many businesses perish on the journey. Don't light up a cigarette, but think of Marlboro and what it had to contend with on its way to hyperprofitability. It knew how to maintain an attack— proving it was willing to stand by its brand—and its cowboys and horses.

Everything seems to be like magic when you mount an attack, stay with it, see the attack turn in your favor, and realize that all along you knew what it took—commitment. You aren't surprised when commitment works, just as you're not surprised when the sun rises.

I feel honor bound to let you know that in all of marketing, the most money is lost due to wonderful marketing programs being abandoned before they had a change to flex their muscles.

Step 9: All about Keeping Track

Many of the weapons you employ will zoom right to the center of the target. Good for you! Other weapons you fire will be aimed at that same target but miss it by a mile. No problem, there's a way around your poor results. It's called keeping track, knowing the bull's-eyes from the misses. By keeping track, you'll be able to get twice as much firepower from your winners and avoid losing a dime on the losers.

One of the ways to keep track is to ask each customer where they first heard of you. Another way is to make tracking part of your system. Whenever you complete a receipt, be sure that the source of the sale is listed. That way each one of your associates is part of the tracking team. Remember this: You may be losing half your marketing investment. The trick is to know which half. And the real trick is never to lose the same half twice.

Step 10: All about Improving

You've done all the work you had to do to launch a successful guerrilla marketing attack. You've got the right plan, the right calendar, the right weapons, and the right attitude. Now what? Now, begin to improve your marketing attack. Using the new knowledge that you gained as your birthright as a guerrilla, improve your message by making it stronger, improve your media by getting a better reach and frequency without paying more for them, improve your budget by investing less in marketing, and improve your results by earning more profits from that diminishing investment.

Your competitors are getting smarter about marketing every day. They're reading the books, subscribing to the newsletters, attending the seminars, taking the courses, listening to the teleseminars, and playing the CDs that are chock full of wisdom. But are they taking

THE TEN-STEP GUERRILLA MARKETING ATTACK

To quickly review, here is a complete list of the ten-steps in a guerrilla marketing attack.

1. Research everything
2. Write benefits list
3. Select weapons and prioritize
4. Create a marketing plan
5. Design a marketing calendar

6. Find fusion marketing partners
7. Launch an attack in slow motion
8. Maintain the attack
9. Keep track through measurement
10. Improve in every area

action based upon what they're learning? Are they developing the aptitudes and embracing the attitudes of the guerrilla?

Chances are, you've got a good head start on them even though you yourself are just at the start-up phase with your marketing. Because you're armed with a plan and know the value of commitment, you've got the upper hand. Now keep it.

■　■　■　■　■

The Guerrilla Entrepreneur's Life Is a Love Story, for Love Illuminates the Way of the Guerrilla

We are delighted to have had the privilege of leading you into the land of marketing certainty and profitability. Our goal was to teach you to walk before you learn to run, and to be sure that you're walking in the right direction, aware of both the minefields and the goldfields. We've done all we can to simplify the process of making your dreams come true.

Those dreams can come true with guerrilla marketing. All you've got to do is start. Now you can. We'll be with you all the way in the form of the nuggets we've generously scattered throughout these pages so they can stick to the ribs of your mind.

—Jay and Jeannie

DEDICATION

Since this book is about start-ups, we would like to dedicate this book to those who have influenced our most important start-up . . . *life itself*! So this book is dedicated to our family tree from whose roots have sprouted the wisdom contained within these pages.

Jay Conrad Levinson

Jay's Grandparents

Jacob Levinson
Stella Levinson
Samuel Cohen
Gertrude Cohen

Jeannie Marie (Rice/Matti) Huffman-Levinson

Jeannie's Grandparents

Fredrick Jacob Matti
Lauretta Ann (O'Mara) Matti
Walter Albert Schulz
Louise Wilhemina (Bauman) Schulz
Charles Oscar Peckham
Gertrude Joanna (Streeter) Peckham
Harry Henry Rice
Mary Elisabeth (Boomer) Rice

Jay's Parents
Robert Reuben Levinson
Sadelle (Cohen) Levinson
Charlie Jacobs
Joe Kovoloff

Jay's Siblings
Myrna Lynne (Levinson) Pope and
Harold Pope

Jay's Nieces and Nephews
Robert Micheal Pope
Gina (Pope) Mandel and Joel
    Mandel (Michael, Jason)
Nicole (Pope) Wagner and
    Eric Wagner (Jade, Natalia)
Corliss "Corky" (Meyerson)
    Fields (John)
Laurence "Larry" Meyerson
Mitchell "Mitch" Meyerson
George Reskin and Peggy
    (Clancy) Reskin
(Beth, Jon, Susan, Maggie)
Melinda (Meyerson) Miller
    and Hal Miller
(Kimberly, Kathleen)

Jay's Aunts, Uncles, and Cousins
Natalie Cohen (Marsha)

Jay's Aunts, Uncles, and Cousins
Lillian (Cohen) Warshauer
    and Sidney Warshauer
    (Myron , Gale Fischer)

Jeannie's Parents
Donald Fredrick Matti
Ruth Louise (Schulz) Matti
Alma Elizabeth (Peckham) Rice
Joseph George Rice Sr.

Jeannie's Siblings
Linda Louise (Matti) Statt and
    Richard Statt
James Donald Matti and
    Amanda (Dearing) Matti
Marianne (Rice Ford) Crossman and
    Don Crossman
Debra Jo (Rice) Capple and
    Thomas Capple
Karen Lee (Rice,Tapia,) Stough and
    Leon Stough
Sandra Lyn (Rice) Borquez
Pamela Sue (Rice,Wood) Reid
    and Don Reid
Lisa Kay (Rice) Smadi and
    Mithkal Smadi
Joseph George "Joey" Rice Jr. and
    Kim Rice
Kenneth Harrison Ford Sr.

Jeannie's Nieces and Nephews
Glenn and Vianna Reskin (CJ,
    Pumahana, Leilana)   Chuck &
Ryan Patrick Statt and Cheryl
    Wilston (Mackenzie, Tyler)

Jeannie's Nieces and Nephews
Kevin Michael Statt
Austin James Matti
Alyssa Dearing Matti

Jay's Aunts, Uncles, and Cousins

May (Alexander) Warshauer

Jerry and Sylvia Cohen
(Howard, Ellen)

Sidney and Gertrude Levinson
(Richard Lee)

Irene and David Basofin
(Jerry, Sharon)

Gertrude and John Solomon
(June)

Leo Levinson
(Mark Levinson)

Jeannie's Nieces and Nephews

Natalie Layla Smadi

Melanie Yasmine Smadi

Jana McCollum (Elijah, Savannah)

Zachary Hekmet Smadi

Ronald "Bubba" Huffman Jr. and
Mary Huffman (Amanda ,Blake,
Austin, Kailyn)

Shayna Dugan and Mathew
Overstreet

Ricky Button

Kenny Eunice (Chelsea, Samantha)

Jeannie's Nieces and Nephews

Kenneth Ford Jr.and Sayoko (Foley)
Ford (Nicole)

Melissa Jean (Ford, Fox) Naugle and
Jimmy Naugle Jr. (Matthew,
Kenny, Jonathan Fox)

Donald "Donnie" Crossman

Michelle (Crossman) Avery and
James Phillips (Dakota Avery,
Sarah Phillips)

Chris Capple and Josie Pinegar
(baby)

Angela (Tapia) Moore and
Andrew Moore (Jaden, Madison,
Jackson Moore)

Gilbert Daniel "Danny" Tapia

Michael Rice and Rachel (Beard)
Rice (baby)

Jennifer Borquez and Bryan Manley

Joseph Wood IV and Stacy (Gerbig)
Wood (Anthony, Robert, Nicolas)

Dylan Stephans

Tina Huffman (Megan, Lauren)

Eric Reid and Angela Jiminez

Dana (Huffman) Deloch and Mike
Deloch (Michael, Dalton, Layton)

Jeannie's Aunts, Uncles, and Cousins

James Schulz and Ruth (Barko) Schulz, Larry and Barb Schulz (Daniel
Schulz) , Nancy (Schulz) Hutchinson and Durward Hutchinson, (Eric,
Ryan Hutchinson) Kathy (Schulz) Kiran and Jay Kiran,

Elenore (Peckham) Marks and Richard Marks, Charles Marks and Teresa
(Bretch) Marks (Jesse, Jason), Roxanne (Marks) Skyvara and Jeffry Skyvara (Francis, Kathleen, Mary Skyvara), Paul Marks and Diana (Lake)
Marks (Steven Marks), Charlene Marks, Helen (Marks) Waldron and Gar-
rett Waldron (Stacey, Melisa Earl)

Jay and Jeannie's Children

Amelia "Amy" Malka Levinson and Les McGhee

Virginia "Ginger" Leigh (Huffman) Adkins and Franklin Delano Adkins III

Daniel "Jeremy" Huffman and Samantha Crystal (Elson) Huffman

Christy Marie Huffman and Wendy DeJesus

Joshua James Huffman and Brandilynn Lavoice Wood

Susan "Celeste" (Huffman, Hogan) Lawrence

Robert Franklin (Huffman) Hogan and Sheryl Wilson

Michael David (Huffman) Hogan and Tonya Hogan

Jay and Jeannie's Grandchildren

Sage Leila Schofield, Seth Meyer Robert Pickett, Natalie Sofia "Ramona" Smith, Annabelle Rose Schofield

Austin Pasquale, Blake Anthony and Cali Rose Adkins

Steven, Michelle Ann and Heidi Mae Livernois

Elexa Leigh, Hayley Nichole, Zachary Kyle, and Jon-Thomas Robert Huffman

Ava Victoria, Alyssa Leigh, Leighton James, and Caden Riley Huffman

Stephan and Stephanie Lawrence

Ashleigh Elizabeth, Sabrina Anne, Amanda Grace, Justin Robert and Hunter Hubert Hogan

Kayla and Megan Hogan

In-Laws

Edwin and Marion Meyerson, Marvin and Shirley (Meyerson) Reskin, Doris and Joseph Schofield, George and Molly Pickett, Jacky Collie and David Smith, Grace (Howard) Huffman, Agnes and George Joyner (Wanda), Thelma and Clarence Howard (David), James and Evelyn Howard (Greg, Alan, Lisa) Diane (DiMasi) Nease and Steve Nease (Carmen , Stevie Nease), Rose DiMasi, Pasquale and Filomena DiMasi,(100 yrs old) Jason Laviolette, Robert Riker and Susan Kossoff (Shawna , Christy Riker), John Elson, Alan Kossoff, Tina Soba, Patti (Jackson) Burton (Steven, Charlene, Angela), Renee Livernois (Salina, Alisha), Kelly Taylor (Brandon), Sherri and Earnest Johnson, Ron Huffman, Bonnie and Allan McCollum, Gary and Deborah Cumby (Billy), Marie Cush and Ellis McGhee, Bertha Visser

Extras

Pat (Meyerson) Levinson, Robert "Frank" Huffman and Sonya, Peter Schofield and Deb (Kahn) Schofield, Bill Pickett, Bryan Smith, Heather Deann (Livernois) Huffman, Amber Iditarod (Taylor) Huffman, Ray Taylor, Wesley Burton, James Wood, John Lawrence, Tamara (Martin) Hogan, Frank "Pic" and Adkins Jr. and Rose (Scott, Chris, April, James), Paul Laviolette, Carol Nease, Enrico "Eddie" Aprea, Michelle (Brookyn), Robert Cumby, Robert Huffman, John Gunter, Josie, Donnie Crosby, Patty Thompson, Robin and Wallace Hogan (William Dane), Alfonse Eunice, Mitzy Eunice, Mary Reskin, Elenore Meyerson, Penny Meyerson, Laura (Johnson) Meyerson, Laurie (Ashner) Meyerson, Marty Fields, Gilbert Tapia, Oscar Madrid, Michael Rodriquez, Floyd Borquez, Duane Avery, Coe Emmett, Edward Guerrero, James Fox, Christina Kelly, Joseph Wood III, David Earl, Allen Polcovich

GLOSSARY OF COMMON MARKETING TERMS

This section contains some commonly used marketing terms and is included to help you when planning your marketing campaigns.

ADI (Area of Dominant Influence). A concept that defines television and radio markets by grouping all counties in which the home market stations receive a preponderance of viewing or listening. Used in measuring the effectiveness of advertising. Can be defined on several levels such as global, national, regional, metro, urban, suburban, or rural.

Ad Specialties. Useful items imprinted with the name of the advertiser and given free to prospects/customers with no obligation. Examples include shirts, hats, pens, mugs, etc.

Advertising. Any paid form of nonpersonal presentation and promotion of ideas, goods, or services by an identified sponsor. May be either print or media. Print advertising venues include:

- Newspaper
- Magazines
- Catalogs
- Direct mail
- Package stuffers
- Billboards
- Brochures
- Fliers

- Signage
- Miscellaneous inserts
- Electronic media advertising venues include:
  - TV network/cable
  - Internet
  - Radio
  - Infomercial

Advertising Metrics

- *click-through*. The process of clicking through an online advertisement to the advertiser's destination.
- *click-through rate (CTR)*. The average number of click-throughs per hundred ad impressions, expressed as a percentage.
- *conversion rate*. The percentage of visitors who take a desired action.
- *cost-per-action (CPA)*. Online advertising payment model in which payment is based solely on qualifying actions such as sales or registrations.
- *cost-per-click (CPC)*. The cost or cost-equivalent paid per click-through.
- *CPM*. Cost per thousand impressions.
- *customer acquisition cost*. The cost associated with acquiring a new customer.
- *hit*. Request of a file from a web server.
- *hybrid model*. A combination of two or more online marketing payment models.
- *impression*. A single instance of an online advertisement being displayed.
- *page view*. Request to load a single HTML page.
- *pay per click (PPC)*. Online advertising payment model in which payment is based solely on qualifying click-throughs.

- *pay per lead (PPL)*. Online advertising payment model in which payment is based solely on qualifying leads.
- *pay per sale (PPS)*. Online advertising payment model in which payment is based solely on qualifying sales.
- *site stickiness*. The amount of time spent at a site over a given time period.
- *unique visitors*. Individuals who have visited a web site (or network) at least once in a fixed time frame, typically a 30-day period.
- *Web site traffic*. The amount of visitors and visits a web site receives.

Advertising Specifications

- *banner ad*. A graphical web advertising unit, typically measuring 468 pixels wide and 60 pixels tall (i.e., 468 x 60).
- *beyond the banner*. Online advertising not involving standard GIF and JPEG banner ads.
- *button ad*. A graphical advertising unit, smaller than a banner ad.
- *HTML banner*. A banner ad using HTML elements, often including interactive forms, instead of (or in addition to) standard graphical elements.
- *interstitial*. An advertisement that loads between two content pages.
- *pop-up ad*. An ad that displays in a new browser window.
- *pop-under ad*. An ad that displays in a new browser window behind the current browser window.
- *rectangle ad*. Any one of the large, rectangular banner sizes suggested by the IAB.
- *rich media*. New media that offers an enhanced experience relative to older, mainstream formats.
- *skyscraper ad*. An online ad significantly taller than the 120 x 240 vertical banner.
- *text ad*. Advertisement using text-based hyperlinks.

- *surround session*. Advertising sequence in which a visitor receives ads from one advertiser throughout an entire site visit.
- *vertical banner*. A banner ad measuring 120 pixels wide and 240 pixels tall.

Affiliate Marketing

- *affiliate*. The publisher/salesperson in an affiliate marketing relationship.
- *affiliate directory*. A categorized listing of affiliate programs.
- *affiliate forum*. An online community where visitors may read and post topics related to affiliate marketing.
- *affiliate fraud*. Bogus activity generated by an affiliate in an attempt to generate illegitimate, unearned revenue.
- *affiliate marketing*. Revenue sharing between online advertisers/merchants and online publishers/salespeople, whereby compensation is based on performance measures, typically in the form of sales, clicks, registrations, or a hybrid model.
- *affiliate merchant*. The advertiser in an affiliate marketing relationship.
- *affiliate network*. A value-added intermediary providing services, including aggregation, for affiliate merchants and affiliates.
- *affiliate software*. Software that, at a minimum, provides tracking and reporting of commission-triggering actions (sales, registrations, or clicks) from affiliate links.
- *exclusivity*. Contract term in which one party grants another party sole rights with regard to a particular business function.
- *payment threshold*. The minimum accumulated commission an affiliate must earn to trigger payment from an affiliate program.
- *return days*. The number of days an affiliate can earn commission on a conversion (sale or lead) by a referred visitor.
- *super affiliate*. An affiliate capable of generating a significant percentage of an affiliate program's activity.

- *two-tier affiliate program.* Affiliate program structure whereby affiliates earn commissions on their conversions as well as conversions of webmasters they refer to the program.

Audience: In advertising, the total number of people reached by an advertisement or medium. This number is measured by indicators such as GRP , CPM, billing rate.

Business and eBusiness

- *application service provider.* Provider of applications/services that are distributed through a network to many customers in exchange for a stream of smaller payments as opposed to one fixed, upfront price.
- *B2B.* Business that sells products or provides services to other businesses.
- *B2C.* Business that sells products or provides services to end-user consumers.
- *circulation.* The distribution of copies of a print vehicle (including subscriptions, newsstands, controlled, and bulk delivery).
- *column inch.* Standard unit of measurement of advertising space. One column in width and approximately $\frac{1}{14}$-inch in depth, or 14 lines to the column inch. One column inch equals 14 agate lines.
- *disintermediation.* The elimination of intermediaries in the supply chain, also referred to as "cutting out the middlemen."
- *guerrilla marketing.* Unconventional marketing intended to get maximum results from minimal resources.
- *free.* Without monetary cost.
- *first-mover advantage.* A sometimes insurmountable advantage gained by the first significant company to move into a new market.
- *interactive agency.* An agency offering a mix of web design/development, internet advertising/marketing, or e-Business/e-commerce consulting.

- *marketing plan.* The part of the business plan outlining the marketing strategy for a product or service.
- *network effect.* The phenomenon whereby a service becomes more valuable as more people use it, thereby encouraging ever-increasing numbers of adopters.

Content and Community

- *blog.* A frequent, chronological publication of personal thoughts and web links.
- *forum.* An online community where visitors may read and post topics of common interest.
- *moderator.* At a forum, someone entrusted by the administrator to help discussions stay productive and within the guidelines.
- *netiquette.* Short for network etiquette, the code of conduct regarding acceptable online behavior.

Controversial Marketing

- *ad blocking.* The blocking of web advertisements, typically the image in graphical web advertisements.
- *banner blindness.* The tendency of web visitors to ignore banner ads, even when banners contain information visitors are actively looking for.
- *buzzword.* A trendy word or phrase that is used more to impress than explain.
- *cookie.* Information stored on a user's computer by a web site so preferences are remembered on future requests.
- *e-mail spam.* Unwanted, unsolicited e-mail.
- *FFA.* Free-for-all links list, where there are no qualifications for adding a link.
- *incentivized traffic.* Visitors who have received some form of compensation for visiting a site.
- *mousetrapping.* The use of browser tricks in an effort to keep a visitor captive at a site, often by disabling the "Back" button or generated repeated pop-up windows.

- *opt-out*. (1) type of program that assumes inclusion unless stated otherwise. (2) to remove oneself from an opt-out program.
- *pagejacking*. Theft of a page from the original site and publication of a copy (or near-copy) at another site.
- *spam*. Inappropriate commercial message of extremely low value.
- *search engine spam*. Excessive manipulation to influence search engine rankings, often for pages that contain little or no relevant content.
- *trick banner*. A banner ad that attempts to trick people into clicking, often by imitating an operating system message.

Coverage. Percent of households who receive or subscribe to a particular media.

Copy. Any or all of the text elements that are part of an advertisement.

Demographics. In marketing, the vital statistics that describe the characteristics of the market. Examples of demographics include: age, sex, race, religion, occupation, education level, marital status, and economic status. The demographics you must consider depend upon your target market. Sources of demographics include:

- Internet
- Census by geographic data
- *Survey of Buying Power*
- *Sales and Marketing Management Journal*
- *Media Market Guide*

Domain Names:
- *domain name*. Location of an entity on the internet.
- *long domain name*. Domain names longer than the original 26 characters, up to a theoretical limit of 67 characters (including the extension, such as .com).

- *whois*. A utility that returns ownership information about second-level domains.

CPM (cost per thousand). The cost of reaching 1,000 of an intended target audience. Measurement of magazine efficiency.

Formula: CPM = (Cost Per Page x 1,000)/circulation. For example, a magazine with a circulation of 2 million and a per-page rate of $24,000 has a cost per thousand of $12.

(CPM = ($24,000 x 1,000) ÷ 2,000,000 = $12)

Direct Mail Advertising. Printed (or otherwise reproduced) communications that are mailed or distributed to prospects or current customers. Key method for reaching specific audiences. Examples of direct mail advertisements include: letters, postcards, statement enclosures, brochures, catalogs, and booklets.

Direct Marketing. Direct communications with individuals to obtain an immediate response. Mail-order sales are an example of direct marketing.

Display Advertisement. Advertisements that usually contain large type and/or illustrations or photographs and are larger in width than one column.

E-Mail Marketing
- *e-mail*. The transmission of computer-based messages over telecommunication technology.
- *e-mail marketing*. The promotion of products or services via e-mail.
- *e-zine*. An electronic magazine, whether delivered via a web site or an e-mail newsletter.
- *e-zine directory*. Directory of electronic magazines, typically of the e-mail variety.
- *HTML e-mail*. E-mail that is formatted using Hypertext Markup Language, as opposed to plain text e-mail.

- *opt-in e-mail.* E-mail that is explicitly requested by the recipient.
- *pass-along rate.* The percentage of people who pass on a message or file.
- *permission marketing.* Marketing centered around obtaining customer consent to receive information from a company.
- *sig file.* A short block of text at the end of a message identifying the sender and providing additional information about them.
- *viral marketing.* Marketing phenomenon that facilitates and encourages people to pass along a marketing message.

Flat Rate/Open Rate. Advertising that does not offer any discounts. Usually for one-time advertising.

Free Web Site Promotion
- *barter.* To exchange goods or services directly without the use of money.
- *banner exchange.* Network where participating sites display banner ads in exchange for credits which are converted (using a predetermined exchange rate) into ads to be displayed on other sites.
- *button exchange.* Network where participating sites display button ads in exchange for credits which are converted (using a predetermined exchange rate) into ads to be displayed on other sites.
- *text link exchange.* Network where participating sites display text ads in exchange for credits which are converted (using a predetermined exchange rate) into ads to be displayed on other sites.
- *web ring.* A means for navigating a group of related sites primarily by going forward and backward.
- *web site award.* An award given from one web site to another.

GRP (Gross Rating Points). Also known as Target Rating Points. This is the cost per 1,000 impressions reaching 1,000 households.

GRP = Reach x Frequency

Household Penetration. Term used to define coverage within a geographical location. It is expressed as a percent, calculated by dividing circulation by the number of households.

Linking Strategy
- *link checker.* Tool used to check for broken hyperlinks.
- *deep linking.* Linking to a web page other than a site's home page.
- *inbound link.* A link from a site outside of your site.
- *outbound link.* A link to a site outside of your site.
- *reciprocal links.* Links between two sites, often based on an agreement by the site owners to exchange links.

Local Advertising. Also known as retail advertising. Advertising placed by a retailer in a local publication or media, in contrast to general or national advertising by a manufacturer in a national or international medium

Market. Group of people who have certain common identifiable geographic, demographic, or psychographic criteria. Examples include:
- *geographic*: area, region, density
- *demographics*: age, education level, occupation, religion
- *psychographics*: values, lifestyle, involvement, social activity

Marketing Plan. A written document, prepared annually, that contains the basic marketing objectives and strategies for the coming year.

Market Share. Percentage of total sales of a product or industry held by one business.

Medium. A vehicle for carrying an advertising message, such as newspapers, television, internet, etc.

Online Advertising
- *advertising network.* A network representing many web sites in selling advertising, allowing advertising buyers to reach

broad audiences relatively easily through run-of-category and run-of-network buys.

- *caching*. The storage of web files for later re-use at a point more quickly accessed by the end user.
- *frequency cap*. Restriction on the amount of times a specific visitor is shown a particular advertisement.
- *house ad*. Self-promotional ad a company runs on its media outlets to put unsold inventory to use.
- *keyword marketing*. Putting your message in front of people who are searching using particular keywords and keyphrases.
- *rep firm*. Ad sales partner specializing primarily in single-site sales.
- *run-of-network (RON)*. Ad buying option in which ad placements may appear on any pages on sites within an ad network.
- *run-of-site (ROS)*. Ad buying option in which ad placements may appear on any pages on sites of the target site.
- *self-serve advertising*. Advertising that can be purchased without the assistance of a sales representative.
- *sponsorship*. Advertising that seeks to establish a deeper association and integration between an advertiser and a publisher, often involving coordinated beyond-the-banner placements.
- *underdelivery*. Delivery of fewer impressions, visitors, or conversions than contracted for a specified period of time.

Position. Refers to the page on which an advertisement appears in the media and to the placement (left, right, top, bottom) on the page. May be Run-of-Paper (ROP) or Preferred.

- *positioning*. Your niche in the marketplace.
- *preferred position*. Specific pages that are considered to be prime areas viewed by readers. More expensive than ROP.

Promotion. A broad term that encompasses all selling activities, advertising, personal selling, public relations, sales promotion, merchandising, and direct marketing.

Public Relations. The management function that identifies, establishes, and maintains mutually beneficial relationships between an organization and the various public media on whom its success or failure depends. Acts as a voice to the media and the public. Designs activities to favorably direct the opinions of others toward the industry or the specific business.

Publicity. An unpaid message that is prompted by newsworthy activities of the dealership/store. Usually prepared by the company itself, but with no guarantee of inclusion in the medium since it is unpaid. One of the many tools used by those in advertising, marketing, and public relations to generate news coverage.

Rate Card. Folder published by media that provides advertisers with rates, circulation data, mechanical requirements, and other information.

Readership. Also referred to as Reach, this is the estimated number of people who read a particular publication. This number differs from circulation because a reader does not necessarily buy a publication but may be a secondary or tertiary reader of a single copy.

Run-of-Paper (ROP). Advertisement placed in a publication at the discretion of the publisher (as compared to a preferred position). Basically, it is placed wherever a publisher has space for it.

Sales Promotion. Mass communication technique that offers short-term incentives to encourage purchases or sales of a product or service. Examples of sales promotion tools include: cash refunds, sweepstakes, contests, coupons, samples, and other patronage rewards.

Search Engine Marketing
- *description tag.* An HTML tag used by web page authors to provide a description for search engine listings.

- *doorway domain*. A domain used specifically to rank well in search engines for particular keywords, serving as an entry point through which visitors pass to the main domain.
- *doorway page*. A page made specifically to rank well in search engines for particular keywords, serving as an entry point through which visitors pass to the main content.
- *invisible web*. The portion of the web not accessible through web search engines.
- *keyword*. A word used in a performing a search.
- *keyword density*. Keywords as a percentage of indexable text words.
- *keyword research*. The search for keywords related to your web site, and the analysis of which ones yield the highest return on investment (ROI).
- *keywords tag*. META tag used to help define the primary keywords of a web page.
- *link popularity*. A measure of the quantity and quality of sites that link to your site.
- *link text*. The text contained in (and sometimes near) a hyperlink.
- *log file*. File that records the activity on a web server.
- *manual submission*. Adding a URL to the search engines individually by hand.
- *meta tag generator*. Tool that will output META tags based on input page information.
- *meta tags*. Tags to describe various aspects about a web page.
- *pay-per-click search engine*. Search engine where results are ranked according to the bid amount, and advertisers are charged when a searcher clicks on the search listing.
- *search engine optimization*. The process of choosing targeted keyword phrases related to a site, and ensuring that the site places well when those keyword phrases are part of a web search.

- *search engine submission*. The act of supplying a URL to a search engine in an attempt to make a search engine aware of a site or page.
- *search spy*. A perpetually refreshing page that provides a real-time view of actual web searches.
- *title tag*. HTML tag used to define the text in the top line of a web browser, also used by many search engines as the title of search listings.
- *top ten*. The top-ten search engine results for a particular search term.
- *URL*. Location of a resource on the internet.
- *volunteer directory*. A web directory staffed primarily by unpaid volunteer editors.

Secondary Coverage. In radio, the area of the station's signal where reception is good only most of the time.

Signature. A company's logo.

Target Market. That segment of the market that the advertiser identifies as the people to whom marketing and advertising efforts will be directed. Determining the target audience is done by establishing geographic, demographic, and/or psychographic criteria.

Tear Sheet. A copy of an advertisement "torn" from a publication and sent to the advertiser for verification purposes.

Web Design and Marketing
- *above the fold*. The section of a web page that is visible without scrolling.
- *ad space*. The space on a web page available for advertisements.
- *ALT text*. HTML attribute that provides alternative text when non-textual elements, typically images, cannot be displayed.
- *animated GIF*. A graphic in the GIF89a file format that creates the effect of animation by rotating through a series of static images.

- *bookmark*. A link stored in a web browser for future reference.
- *cascading style sheets (CSS)*. A data format used to separate style from structure on web pages.
- *favicon*. A small icon that is used by some browsers to identify a bookmarked web site.
- *Flash*. Multimedia technology developed by Macromedia to allow much interactivity to fit in a relatively small file size.
- *frames*. A structure that allows for the dividing of a web page into two or more independent parts.
- *home page*. The main page of a web site.
- *JavaScript*. A scripting language developed by Netscape and used to create interactive web sites.
- *linkrot*. When web pages previously accessible at a particular URL are no longer reachable at that URL due to movement or deletion of the pages.
- *navigation*. That which facilitates movement from one web page to another web page.
- *shopping cart*. Software used to make a site's product catalog available for online ordering, whereby visitors may select, view, add/delete, and purchase merchandise.
- *site search*. Search functionality specific to one site.
- *splash page*. A branding page before the home page of a web site.
- *web browser*. A software application that allows for the browsing of the World Wide Web.
- *web design*. The selection and coordination of available components to create the layout and structure of a web page.
- *web site usability*. The ease with which visitors are able to use a web site.

Web Hosting

- *anonymous FTP*. An option in FTP that allows users to download files without having to establish and account.
- *Apache*. An open source web server software.

- *ASP hosting*. Web hosting that supports Active Server Pages, a server-side scripting environment from Microsoft.
- *autoresponder*. A program that sends an automatic form response to incoming e-mails.
- *bandwidth*. How much data can be transmitted in a time period over a communications channel, often expressed in kilobits per second (kbps).
- *burstable bandwidth*. A hosting option that allows sites to use the available network capacity to handle periods of peak usage.
- *business hosting*. Web hosting geared towards the mission-critical functions demanded by business-class customers.
- *colocated hosting*. Hosting option whereby the host provides and is responsible for the equipment, dedicating an entire server to the client's web sites.
- *ColdFusion hosting*. Web hosting that supports ColdFusion, a web application language introduced by Allaire and currently owned by Macromedia.
- *data transfer*. The total amount of outbound traffic from a web site, typically measured in gigabytes (Gb).
- *dedicated hosting*. Hosting option whereby the host provides and is responsible for the equipment, dedicating an entire server to the client's web sites.
- *dedicated IP*. An IP address dedicated to a single web site.
- *web hosting*. The business of providing the storage, connectivity, and services necessary to serve files for a web site.

INDEX

BE PART OF THE INNER CIRCLE BY JOINING THE GUERRILLA MARKETING ASSOCIATION

Can you imagine what it would be like if you had direct access to the author of the best selling marketing series in history for less than the cost of a cup of coffee a day? That's only part of what you get when you join the Guerrilla Marketing Association. You are also entitled to:

- *The Guerrilla Marketing Insider.* A monthly online report filled with over 20 cutting-edge marketing tips that are new, actionable, and extremely inexpensive—or even free. Each report includes videos with top marketing people.
- *Coaching.* A one-hour weekly real-time telephone coaching and Q&A session with Jay Conrad Levinson, plus brand name experts and coaches. You can pepper them with questions and get your answers immediately.
- *Guerrilla Marketing Tip of the Day.* A new one is posted on our site every day. It takes under a minute to read and can have a permanent impact. We'll also send you by e-mail *The Guerrilla Marketing Weekly Intelligence.* Good stuff.
- *The Guerrilla Marketing Forum.* Here you can ask any and as many questions as you like. Each will be personally answered by Jay Conrad Levinson or one of his hand-picked Guerrilla Marketing Association coaches, usually within 24 hours. Some of these coaches are paid $1,000 per hour for consulting. But their answers come to you at no extra cost.
- *The Guerrilla Marketing Association Affiliate Program.* Pays you $15 per month for each new member you sign up.
- *Teleclass.* A weekly one-hour teleclass with the Guerrilla Marketing coaches.

Membership in the Guerrilla Marketing Association is only $49.97 per month. That's less than the cost of a cup of coffee a day.

SIGN UP TODAY AND YOUR FIRST MONTH'S MEMBERSHIP IS FREE
www.guerrillamarketingassociation.com

E-MAIL US FOR FREE DIGITAL REPRINTS OF THE 200 GUERRILLA MARKETING WEAPONS
www.gmarketing.com

GUERRILLA MARKETING ASSOCIATION
MEMBERSHIP APPLICATION

___YES, I want to take advantage of this special offer. By acting today, I am entitled to all of the following:

1. Access to the Guerrilla Marketing Association and all its services. I can cancel at any time, no hassles, no questions.
2. The very latest issue of *Guerrilla Marketing Insider*, with valuable marketing tactics and videos.
3. Weekly one-hour teleclass and Q & A phone session with Jay Conrad Levinson, marketing coaches, and guest experts.
4. The Guerrilla Marketing Forum, where Jay and his Association coaches answer your toughest questions.
5. *The Guerrilla Marketing Weekly Intelligence,* which will give you even more ways to raise your profits.
6. Weekly one-hour teleclass with GM coaches designed to answer YOUR questions.
7. A chance to earn residual income as a Guerrilla Affiliate.

My membership fee of $49.97 will be waived the first month and
automatically billed each month after that.

First Name: _____ Last Name: _____

Email: _____ Phone: _____

Street Address: _____

City/State/Zip: _____

Type of card: Visa ❑   MasterCard ❑   AMEX ❑   Discover ❑

Credit Card #: _____ Exp. Date: _____

Username you want: _____

Password you want: _____
(Please note your username and password. You will also receive them with your confirmation of membership to the e-mail address you provided us!)

Signature: _____

How did you hear about us? _____

Mail to: Guerrilla Marketing International 714 Sawyer SE, Olympia, WA 98501

386-791-7479 or join online by going to: www.guerrillamarketingassociation.com